The Light of Discovery

also by Toni Packer:

The Work of This Moment

The Light of Discovery

Toni Packer

with a Foreword by Joan Tollifson

Charles E. Tuttle Co., Inc.
Boston • Rutland, Vermont • Tokyo

First paperback edition published in 1999 by Tuttle Publishing, an imprint of Periplus
Editions (HK) Ltd., with editorial offices at 153 Milk Street, Boston, Massachusetts 02109.

Library of Congress Cataloging-in-Publication Data

Packer, Toni, 1927–
    The light of discovery / by Toni Packer.
       p.   cm.
    ISBN 0–8048–3196–3 (pbk.)
    1. Spiritual life. 2. Meditation. I. Title.
BL624.P22 1995
291.4'4—dc20   95–23229
                                           CIP

Distributed by

USA
Tuttle Publishing
Distribution Center
Airport Industrial Park
364 Innovation Drive
North Clarendon, VT 05759-9436
Tel: (802) 773-8930
Fax: (802) 773-6993

SOUTHEAST ASIA
Berkeley Books Pte. Ltd.
5 Little Road #08-01
Singapore 536983
Tel: (65) 280-3320
Fax: (65) 280-6290

JAPAN
Tuttle Shokai Ltd.
1-21-13, Seki
Tama-ku, Kawasaki-shi
Kanagawa-ken 214, Japan
Tel: (044) 833-0225
Fax: (044) 822-0413

CANADA
Raincoast Books
8680 Canbie Street
Vancouver, British Columbia
V6P 6M9
Tel: (604) 323-7100
Fax: (604) 323-2600

05 04 03 02 01 00 99
1 3 5 7 9 10 8 6 4 2

Printed in the United States of America
Cover by Treetop Design

Contents

Acknowledgments

The Light of Discovery would not have happened without sustained contact with many people in private meetings, group discussions, and correspondence. Heartfelt thanks to our friends for letting us include their letters in this volume; to Susan McCallum for transcribing and pre-editing tapes of talks and for her encouragement to bring out this book; to Joan Tollifson, for transcribing and pre-editing numerous tapes of talks, for making valuable suggestions for the manuscript, and for writing the Foreword; to Carole Sierpien for her help with the computer; to past and present members of the staff at Springwater Center for their help in many ways; to Michael Kerber and Isabelle Bleecker of Charles E. Tuttle Co. for their interest in publishing this volume; and to my husband Kyle for the good times we have had editing and putting this book together.

Foreword by Joan Tollifson

One of the most striking aspects of Toni Packer's talks and writings is the listening presence out of which they emerge. Toni has the courage to put aside all the books, all the authorities, and be with the moment at hand, simply, openly, not knowing what it is or where its going. She's looking anew right now, on the spot. A talk is listening, open space, silence, birdsong, airplane hum, chainsaw buzz, wind, cough, heartbeat, and words. But most importantly it is listening.

Toni is by far the simplest and most radical spiritual teacher I have encountered, radical in the sense of going uncompromisingly to the bare root. She no longer calls herself a teacher because she sees such thought-created conceptual imagery as "teacher" and "student" as obscuring, rather than revealing the truth.

Toni's work involves direct discovery of undivided wholeness, the immediacy of pure being in which there is no sense of separation or limitation. Such immediacy is seeing without knowing, listening and wondering without answers or formulas. The work is also about exposing and clarifying everything that gets in the way of such simple, open being—namely our habitual, conditioned thinking, centered around the imagined "me," and made up of images about ourselves, the others, the world—all of it a picture, an abstraction, habitually mistaken for reality or truth. This obscuration and mistaking of concept for reality is at the root of our human suffering, our wars, our greed, our violence, our addictions. Toni directs attention to what is—*right* now, *this* moment, *right* here—and points out, again and again, in ever subtler ways, the difference between thinking and being.

I remember the first time I heard Toni—a passionate white-haired woman in ordinary, casual clothes, bright colors maybe, nothing that suggested traditional religious attire in any way—talking with her eyes closed, listening so intently, swaying and moving as she talked, as if dancing, reaching for something unimaginably delicate. Listening to her that first time, so many things opened up and became clear, and I am still listening to her.

In meetings with people Toni is direct and open. You are invited to bring up anything you wish to go into, or simply sit quietly together in silence, listening to rain or birds or the ticking of the clock, to whatever thoughts or sensations may arise. Toni meets you as a peer, not as a superior, always questioning the way thought searches for answers and explanations, for methods and techniques. She deflects attempts to romanticize her or turn her into an authority.

In her first book, *Seeing Without Knowing*, published by the Genesee Valley Zen Center in 1983, Toni said, "only in seeing and dropping unequivocally everything that divides us can there be freedom." This statement intrigued me and horrified me. I was drawn to it, I resisted it, I questioned it. We cling tenaciously to who we think we are: gay or straight, man or woman, black or white, leftist or right-winger, pro-life or pro-choice, intellectual or non-intellectual. When I came here certain identities were very important to me. The longer I'm here, the less real they all seem. What matters is something else. Something very simple, very immediate, always here. This possibility of waking up to the truth has global ramifications because our interpersonal scuffles are microcosms of the larger conflicts that divide and ravage the world.

Born in 1927, Toni grew up in Nazi Germany, the daughter of two scientists. Her mother was Jewish, but because of her father's prestigious career, the family was spared from the Holocaust, at least until the very end, when they discovered that their names had been put on the death list. Toni's childhood was a strange blend of bourgeois German life amidst the rising specter of Nazism, world war, bombing raids, fear of death, and the early realization that no one could protect her, that life was apparently meaningless and full of horror.

The family emigrated to Switzerland after the war, where Toni met and married a young American exchange student, Kyle Packer. Toni and Kyle moved to the States in 1951 and settled near Buffalo, New York, where Kyle became a school teacher and eventually a school principal. Toni attended university in Buffalo, she and Kyle adopted a baby, and eventually, in the late sixties, she and Kyle discovered the Zen Center in Rochester.

Toni began attending sesshins (extended meditation retreats) with Roshi Philip Kapleau and soon became his disciple. She was asked by him to counsel students in psychological matters and several years later to assume teaching responsibilities. As time went on, Toni found herself beginning to question the tradition-bound aspects of Zen practice: the hierarchy, the authoritarian teacher-student relationship, the ceremonies, the dogmas—all of which seemed to her to get in the way of simple, effortless presence. She wanted to work not from memory, not from tradition and the past, but rather from an immediacy that cannot be captured by word or image. Coming upon the writings and talks of J. Krishnamurti, Toni found that the profundity of his questioning and insight helped to illuminate what she was struggling with herself. In the early eighties, when Toni was put in charge of the Center, she realized she couldn't continue to work in the traditional way.

In 1981, Toni left the Rochester Zen Center along with a number of the people who were working with her, and together they founded the Genesee Valley Zen Center. Toni had a strong feeling about working in the country where people could be in close contact with the natural world, a world not dominated or produced by human thought. The group purchased several hundred acres of land located an hour south of Rochester and built a retreat center from scratch. The project was done on a shoestring budget by volunteer labor, people often learning as they went along. The first retreats in rural Springwater were held in the spring of 1985.

There is something powerful and vast here on this land, in wind, weather, seasons, wildlife, open space—something infinitely richer and more real than the cardboard constructions of thought, which seem pale and flat in comparison. Nature is vibrant and amazing, and it is here in this ever-changing and organic place that Toni has chosen to base her work.

In time, the Genesee Valley Zen Center became Springwater Center. The word Zen was dropped, Toni no longer called herself a teacher, the traditional Zen emphasis on posture and form fell away, people stopped wearing Zen robes and began sitting more frequently in chairs as well as on cushions on the floor, and sitting in an armchair became as acceptable as the lotus position. Toni stopped using koans (Zen riddles) and formal inquiries in working with people, group meetings were introduced into retreats in addition to the private individual meetings with Toni, untimed sittings were experimented with, things got simpler and more open. There has been a steady movement away from the rigidity and athletic qualities of traditional Zen practice, a movement toward shorter sittings, more comfortable postures. But through all these shifts in style, the essence of Toni's work and the acuity of her vision has remained very much the same.

Today the Center holds approximately ten silent retreats a year, most of them with Toni. The place is singularly unambitious and spare. There are no workshops in brush painting or archery, no major annual fund drives, no daily meditation schedule outside of retreat, no promises, no fanfare, no priesthood, no slick packaging. There is a sobriety here, an unseductive austerity that rings true and comes with warmth and affection and good-heartedness. This is a place where people can come to be quiet, to do and be nothing, a rarity in our busy world today. It is a place where people can look, alone and together, at what is arising in all of us, perhaps not having to take it personally, but seeing it as it really is, as one whole happening without any separate, individual actors. Images about self and others can become transparent and fall away. The work is arduous and infinitely subtle, and at the same time effortless and utterly simple.

Toni now spends roughly half the year in Springwater and the rest of the year traveling, giving retreats in California, Germany, Holland, Sweden, and Poland, and people from all around the world appear in Springwater to attend retreats and meet with her here in this quiet place.

What is said here in this book is not presented with the "closure of authority," as Toni put it recently, but is rather "something to be considered, questioned, wondered about, taken further." There is a tremendous subtlety and depth in Toni's words that can be easily missed in quick, analytical reading. Open listening is another mode entirely.

Joan Tollifson
March 1995
Springwater, New York

To the Reader

Since the publication of *The Work of This Moment** there have been many requests for another book to cover more topics, to shed light on our day-to-day living, at home, in relationships, at work, in school, in love, in thought, in grief, in therapy, in retreat, and in meditation.

The response is *The Light of Discovery,* a compilation of essays, articles published in issues of the *Springwater Center Newsletter,* correspondence, excerpts from talks given in and out of retreat, conversations, and interviews, all freshly edited or re-written for this publication.

Written words can be read quickly to satisfy the roving intellect with its unceasing hunger for more knowledge. Another way of approaching *The Light of Discovery* is to read meditatively, using a chapter, a paragraph, or maybe just a single sentence to wonder and examine what is being said—questioning and listening inwardly into who is questioning, and probing inwardly into what the words may actually be pointing at.

We are not normally aware of the extent to which all of us live deeply enmeshed in a vast network of conditioned thoughts, images, assumptions, prejudices, beliefs, and so on, all accompanied by complex physical sensations and reactions that affect the total organism. We continuously perceive and create ourselves, each other, and our "world," according to these conditioned images and beliefs, and we automatically defend our perception of the truth about how things really are.

What is truth?

Can there be a pause in this vast stream of conditioned thinking and reacting, a quiet inward looking and listening without knowing that may disengage the momentum of the past while shedding light on it?

Not answering yes or no, can we find out directly?

---

*published in 1990.

The Light of Discovery

Expectation

*In the expectation of wonderful things to happen in the future,
one doesn't hear the sound of the wind and rain, the breath and
heartbeat this instant.*

Is there an expectation in the mind right now that reading this will do
something for one? Is there an expectation that something helpful may
happen, maybe something that will resolve one's problems? Instead,
can there be *awareness* of that expectation? Is expectation blocking open
awareness of what is going on right now, this very instant? It's a simple
question. Can we hold it a moment, looking carefully, feeling expectation actively engaging the mindbody?

Expectation is the idea of getting something, becoming something.
Is there a feeling like that? It is not only mental; it is also physical. It is
thought, a fantasy, a whole inner physical movement toward something
and at the same time away from something.

If I expect something to happen, can I be aware of how this idea affects the whole organism I call "me"? Let's take some time with this,
sounding it out internally. If I think something marvelous will happen,
that expectation triggers tremendous energy throughout the body,
doesn't it? I noticed as a child that anticipating my birthday party made
me feel wonderfully happy for a long time. The party itself never quite
measured up to the expectations—the day was over and gone so fast!
Was I really there with what was actually happening, or was I just continuing the dream about a dream?

In the expectation of wonderful things to happen in the future, one
doesn't hear the sound of the wind and rain, the breath and heartbeat
this instant. Fantasy provides stimulation. When fantasizing, one

---

This chapter was adapted from a retreat talk and published in the Springwater
Center Newsletter *of April 1993.*

imagines pleasant past and future experiences, for example, imagining what will happen on the coming weekend when I'm with my friend. Can we see that fantasy creates constant new stimulation that drowns out the lack of stimulation right now? And what is *that?*

Boredom? What one labels "boredom," one does not take the time or energy to experience directly. After all, everybody knows what boredom is. But do we really? What is it? Have we ever taken the time to wonder about it? What is boredom when the label is put aside? There are sensations throughout the body. There may be a very flat, dull state and also a certain restlessness from wanting something else, something more exciting, a new and different stimulation. This is not just mental or verbal stuff: the whole body craves its accustomed "fix." The process is like addiction and withdrawal—feeling deprived and wanting, wanting, wanting.

Is this what is actually going on? Can one quietly discover all these subtle movements in oneself? Can I, for this moment, just listen quietly?

We rarely touch *this.* We rarely contact this simple moment. So used to constant input and excitement, we lack fine-tuning into all the subtleties of this instant, the ability to register a quiet aliveness without the stirring of expectation.

It's simple to listen quietly, yet it's not easy, because there is a tremendous momentum of habit to create stimulation through fantasy. This is particularly noticeable when we're removed from our daily life during retreat, when we are without our accustomed morning-till-night stimulation—no excitement through the media, through relationships, work, noise, music, entertainment, movies.

One person commented that getting home after a retreat, she felt depressed. Her habitual reaction to depressed feelings had been to get an inspiring book or tape, but this time she didn't do that. She just remained quietly with what she had called "depression" and realized for the first time that reading a book or listening to a tape was dealing only with *thoughts*—trying to straighten out her thoughts about herself. Being *directly* with the "inner stuff" was something that had never happened before. This experience was entirely new and different—alive— this was no longer "depression."

To really be with the raw stuff of this moment doesn't need identification or labelling. We don't need to know it. Just *being* has nothing to do with expectation. It has nothing to do with a goal. Having a goal is already moving away. From what? What are we moving away from?

We think we can't bear it—the boredom, the depression, the pain. We feel it's too awful, too difficult. It's not the "spiritual work" we imagine. But these are all thoughts, feelings, labels.

What is the real thing—this instant of not expecting anything?

Why Attach a Name to What Is?

Insight reveals self-centered thoughts and images for what they are, and when the truth of "self" is laid bare, "self"-enclosing thoughts abate. Life is a vast, unknowable movement of wholeness with no one separate from it and nothing outside of it.

QUESTIONER: What is it like to have a day-to-day, moment-to-moment relationship with God, or, if you like, spiritual forces? More specifically, can you describe the nature of this personal relationship, how you have cultivated it, and how it manifests in your day-to-day life?

TONI: Rather than immediately looking for an answer, can we carefully examine the question? The question assumes that there is an individual entity, "me," who has a personal relationship with "God" or spiritual forces outside of itself, and that this relationship can be cultivated. Despite our millennia-old ideas and convictions about a separate "self," is there really any such thing?

Can we thoroughly question this sense of separation into "me" and "you," "me" and "God"—not just intellectually, but deeply, meditatively wondering what is this sense of "self" with its feelings of isolation, fear, and want? What is it?

Can there be silent questioning, listening inwardly without knowing?

And what is God? Can we look at it together? Can we start by examining what the word "God" may evoke within us?

For those of us who were brought up in a theistic tradition, the concept carries conditioned mental and emotional meanings and reactions, doesn't it? These vary from one human being to the next. We all have different personal histories; this is a universal fact.

The question was submitted to Toni in an October 1989 letter requesting her to write an article on the subject. It was published in the Springwater Center Newsletter *of January 1990.*

As a child, deeply impressed by Old Testament stories and illustrations of God's rewards as well as His punitive actions, by His frightful wrath as well as His comforting protection, I felt I had to be obedient, good, and repentant in order to reap the benefits of God's protection. "God" was unquestionably an entity outside of "me" that needed to be carefully heeded, placated, and pleased in order to avoid incurring His violent wrath.

Stories about the love of God manifesting in His sending His son into this world to take its sins upon Himself were somewhat comforting. But I never experienced the promised relief from sorrow and guilt. Growing up in Germany during the Hitler years with a Jewish mother and a Gentile father, I felt under the imminent threat of persecution, and, with the ever increasing violence and destruction, the insanity of war, my belief in a loving God who could allow all this to happen collapsed. I felt the depth of this doubt most vividly after a severe air raid. What arose amidst the smoldering shambles was the nagging question "What is the meaning of this utterly meaningless life?"

This question, with its unsettling effects, remained with me into the postwar years, through my marriage to an American, the study of psychology, sociology, and anthropology at an American university, the adoption of a baby, family life, and the reading of a lot of books on psychotherapy, mythology, and Eastern religions. Eventually I took up Zen training and found insight, relief, and strength in quiet sitting and koan work.

Later coming upon the teachings of J. Krishnamurti, I experienced the thorough falling away of belief in traditional religious constructs, both the old and the newly acquired ones. It became clear that even while one is engaged in serious spiritual training, thought keeps creating new constructs to which it becomes unwittingly attached.

It was also clear that our most beloved construct is the separate entity called "myself," "me." The deeply conditioned belief in the true existence of this "self" and the attachment to it turn out to be the rootsource of our sense of isolation, with its sorrow, insufficiency, aggrandizement, fear, wanting, guilt.

To assuage our fears and provide a semblance of security and meaning, thought and imagination invent belief systems, rituals, and paths to salvation. But thought and imagination do not and cannot overcome the basic limitation of thought. Belief in being separate and in being able to find meaning and salvation can only end in the direct insight that this is *belief*. Belief creates the separation, and with it the need for meaning and salvation. When belief dissolves, there is no one to save. This realization brings joy beyond words.

Being caught up in ideas and images about a separate "me" is like living in a small capsule among other capsules, with all the conflicts and sorrow that capsule living brings. One wonders about the meaning of living that way, and, in fact, there is no meaning to it. The part can never see the whole. Thought can invent ideas and fantasies about something meaningful, something whole, divine, something beyond, and try to establish a relationship with that, but this remains a relationship between thoughts and images—"me" and "my God."

But this isn't "my story" when the "I" is not the center—then there is only the story of humankind. When it begins to dawn on us that the "world" isn't the way we have imagined it to be, thought throws up disturbing doubts about "me and the world," and the "God beyond." Despair manifests as the meaning of life collapses. Will one continue to invent solace? Will one attach oneself to other people's words or become cynical and give up altogether? Or will there be the awakening of a deep questioning within—inquiring patiently, thoroughly, without knowing the answer?

We may think we know, but knowing comes from memory, and memory isn't immediate insight. What is needed is a thorough questioning from scratch, a fresh looking, a pure awareness without judgment. Insight dissolves the capsule of separation. Only then can there be love and compassion.

How this happens is not knowable by thought even though thought invents theories and systems about it. But theories and systems are not insight. Insight reveals self-centered thoughts and images for what they are, and when the truth of "self" is laid bare, "self"-enclosing thoughts abate. Life is a vast, unknowable movement of wholeness with no one separate from it and nothing outside of it. "Inside" and "outside" are thought-created divisions. Wisdom, love, and compassion are not the invention of thought, nor are they products or the properties of anyone. They operate mysteriously, without cause and conflict, when "self"-thoughts are illuminated freely.

At the time of inattention, thought is busily at work in its narrow, conditioned space: wanting, fearing, inventing, grasping, hoping, striving, judging, condemning, or accepting. Undivided awareness illumines *the whole thing*. Illumination is the ending of the sense of separation.

Will inattention take over again? Thought wants to predict everything, to make sure and be secure for all *time*. But time itself is a creation of thought.

Can there simply be stillness without knowing? This stillness, this pure awareness, with its wisdom and compassion—is this the manifestation of God from moment to moment? Who knows? Where does the question itself come from? The word, the name, is not *what is*. What is is without self. It is unknowable, unthinkable, indivisible. Why attach a name to what is?

Action Without Effort

But no-self is not a concept or an entity; it is a state of immediate, undivided awareness, presence. And in that presence the entire circuit of self-centeredness is illumined. This is attention.

QUESTIONER: I feel that you have clarified for me the question "Who is it that is aware?" After listening to you, I have come to see that the "me" or "I" is an illusion—just a bundle of thoughts, memories, and emotions. But when one decides, as an example, not to overeat, or when one decides to clean out the garage (despite not feeling like doing so) —who or what is deciding to do or not to do these things? When a person uses "self-discipline" or "goal setting," or "determination" or "willpower"—who or what is doing the "willing"?

Granted that there is no "self," whence comes the idea of "self-discipline" or "willpower"? Why is it that some children (and adults, of course) have "self-control" and others appear to have very little "self-control?" What is this "no-self" that has "self-control?"

TONI: Is there really clear insight into the fact that the "self" is an illusion, or is it an intellectual understanding? Will an intellectual understanding, even when clear and convincing, resolve your questions?

There is danger in using the label "illusion" when referring to the self. The brain may associate the word "illusion" with religious ideas propounding the unreality of the world of the senses. "Illusion" also implies something "wrong," something we must be free of. So the label does not help us to see and to understand directly what constitutes the "self"—self-centeredness—in our moment-to-moment living. Is that clear?

This question was submitted in a note to Toni. The article was written for the Springwater Center Newsletter *of October 1987.*

To understand self-centeredness directly, we need to be aware of the self-image, and not just of one image, but the arising and functioning of many self-images. We have a strong conviction that these images are solid and real, that they are palpable, physical sensations. They feel like "me," but what am I *really*? As long as self-images with all their associated bodily feelings and emotions keep operating undetected, they constantly deceive me, masquerading as a solid entity I feel to be "me." The "me" seems to be the driving force behind making decisions, behind willing and resisting, the power behind fearing, wanting, striving, achieving, or failing. Can we pause for a moment to wonder and look carefully at all this?

You ask, who or what is doing the willing, the deciding not to overeat or to clean out the garage. Let's look at it together. The garage needs cleaning out, that's clear. The idea/feeling "I don't want to do it. It's so unpleasant" brings in the "me." The thought/feeling "I must go ahead with it whether I like it or not" is also felt to be "me," isn't it? It feels like a battle between two "me's"—the resisting one and the disciplined one. But what is actually going on? Isn't there just an alternating, conflicting series of ideas, feelings, and energies either gridlocked, or vacillating back and forth, or one winning out over the other?

What is doing the willing, the deciding, the acting? If we drop the idea that a solid entity is behind these acts, how will we tackle these questions? Until now we have assumed that there is an "I" that decides and wills. But now we don't know what the exact process is anymore. Can we put aside what we think we know or what we thought we knew? Are we actually at the point of not knowing, or do we only verbally profess not to know? There is a great difference between these two states.

Let us look at this carefully. Are we expecting verbal answers? That means that the brain remains in the mode of "wanting to know," waiting to find answers. But if the brain is truly not knowing, it is no longer searching for verbal, intellectual answers. Rather it is quiet—openly attentive to what is taking place. Now what is this "I must not overeat," and "I ought to clean out the garage," and "I don't feel like it"? Isn't it just a series of alternating ideas popping up and triggering all kinds of different energies?

Can there be a new and fresh awareness, without *judgment* of what is happening automatically throughout the mindbody from moment to moment? Let's see.

We want to find out how the "decision" not to eat that extra helping of food comes into being. Observing carefully, there is the physical pleasure of eating and the thought-feeling "I would like more of that." Then there are opposing ideas: "I shouldn't eat more. It's not good for me. It's greed. I must control myself. I must pay more attention." And there are the physical sensations accompanying all those ideas. When there is merely a battle of ideas going on inside, the one carrying more pleasure or more energy of persuasion wins out—one will continue to eat more, or one will stop. Then the thought comes up: "I'm glad I had the willpower to stop," or "I wish I had the willpower not to overeat!" The process goes on and on and on—more thoughts and more conflicting sensations and feelings accompanying them. No thought occurs without accompanying bodily sensations, feelings, and emotions. We live in a succession of crisscrossing thoughts with their physical orchestrations, all of which are creating and maintaining the sense of "me." Can we see this directly, at least have a glimpse into what's going on?

Thoughts generate tremendous energies to do something or not to do something, to get somewhere, to control or to inhibit action. Can there be insight into the power of thought? Where is the "I" in all this? Is it just a powerful thought?

What about "self-discipline" and "self-control"? To ask, "What is this 'no-self' that has 'self-control'?" is putting the wrong question, isn't it? It is making a *new entity* out of the concept of "no-self." But no-self is not a concept or an entity; it is a state of immediate, undivided awareness, presence. And in that presence the entire circuit of self-centeredness is illumined. This is attention. Attention without self-center can illuminate self-centeredness. It sounds paradoxical, but only thought creates conundrums.

In open awareness without a self-center, things are simply seen for what they are—everything is happening on its own. Cleaning out the garage or not overeating cease to be problems. What needs to be done is clear and gets done, or it doesn't get done. When the energy of clarity takes the place of resistance, action flows freely, without effort.

What Is This Work?

When this open listening happens, thought does not intrude,
because thought is not needed. The immediacy of being needs
no thought.

JOAN: Suppose people come here for a meditation retreat and they ask
you, "What is this work?" What would you say to them?

TONI: The essence is to come upon a profound kind of listening and
openness that reveals the intense power and momentum of our human
conditioning, how we are caught up and attached to ideas about ourselves and each other, how violently we defend these ideas—not just individually but collectively—and how this defense keeps us isolated
from each other and from ourselves. The other aspect of this listening
is to come upon an inner/outer silence—stillness—spaciousness in
which there is no sense of separation or limitation, outside or inside.

JOAN: If I want to see through these ideas that I'm creating and ar-
rive at this more open and spacious place, what should I do?

TONI: Can we start where we are and not attempt to get someplace?
That is another idea, the idea of "an open space." What is going on
right now? Does wanting to be in an open place arise because one has
heard about an open place and is feeling closed up inside? Can there be
an immediate listening to where we are now—wanting open spaces—
and also hear the birds singing at the same time, the breathing that is
going on? We get caught up with the idea of where we want to be and
are oblivious to what is actually going on right now.

JOAN: Suppose I see the same patterns coming up year after year,
habits that I feel stuck in. It might be addiction to caffeine or some other substance. It might be habitual patterns of thought like obsessively

The following interview with Toni by Joan Tollifson was conducted in the fall
of 1993 at Springwater. Joan Tollifson is a staff member of the Springwater Center.

thinking about the future. I see it over and over, but it keeps happening, and I can't get out of it.

TONI: When you say, "I see it, but I can't get out of it," what is the quality of that seeing? Here is where you really need to look and examine carefully. Is it *thinking* about your habit-patterns—how long they have persisted, how this is never going to end, wanting to know how to fix it? This is not seeing. This is thinking. It's not an on-the-spot discovery of thought arising. To *see* the thought of wanting freedom as it arises is different from *thinking*, "I've had this thought pattern all my life, and nothing has happened about it, and what can I do about it?"

JOAN: It seems that one pattern is being seen—thoughts about the future, for example—and then immediately a new train of thought takes over: "This just keeps happening, and I can't get out of it."

TONI: Yes, one is discovering not just the thought of the future, but also the next thought: "I wish I didn't have these thoughts." There is a brief gap between the two thoughts. First there's the thought about the future, then waking up to the fact that this thought arose a moment ago, and the instantaneous resuming of thoughts—"Why do I have these thoughts, I wish I would be free of them"—which is the end of awareness and the continuation of thinking.

JOAN: Toni, what do you mean by thinking? Some people might say that they have tremendous feelings of anger coming up that are coming out of nowhere. They're not thinking about anything.

TONI: The assertion that an overpowering emotion comes out of nowhere may not be based on direct observation. There cannot be direct observation if one insists that one knows the emotion comes out of nowhere, that it is strictly an emotion. But if one is interested in what anger is, not approaching it with a motive of getting rid of it or justifying it, but wondering about this whole process of anger, then one will begin to watch. Maybe one will see that thought or remembrance of an incident can bring the whole mindbody into a state of agitation—violent feelings and images of retaliation. It is an intertwined network of thoughts, ways in which we describe to ourselves what is happening, memories of how we have been treated or talked to—maybe as little children—and the angry response to not wanting to be treated like this.

One begins to see the total interrelationship of thought and the emotions that are manifested in the body. Thought is a tremendously complex thing that involves every fiber of the body, with bodily feelings creating more thoughts and those thoughts creating more feelings.

Right now there is a sound. Thought can represent it as a bird call, and that thought may cause a reaction: I like birds or I don't. Can one hear those thoughts, and also the sound, which is not thought? What is it?

JOAN: So this work is listening, listening to the sounds like the bird and the airplane, to the thoughts going through the mind (like "I wonder if I'm experiencing this moment as fully as I should be"), feeling the sensations in the body. Is that how you see the work?

TONI: Yes. And there is a *spaciousness* in this listening, all the senses open. One is not trying to grasp or reject anything. Or if grasping, rejecting, or judging happens, can *that* be perceived spaciously, so that whatever is happening happens in an open space of no judgment? A judgment that arises need not be judged further. One need not try to get rid of it. There is space for *everything* to happen. Can we simply be with *whatever* is here, not as a judge or doer or controller, but as a listening space—the stillness of it all, the spaciousness, the energy?

JOAN: I notice that thought starts to turn this into a project or a practice, in which I'm trying to do this.

TONI: What is the trying? Can we look at this? What are the ingredients of trying? You mentioned one—thought turning what has just been said about listening openly into a project: "I have to do this. This is my task to do all the time." Can one hear such thoughts going on?

JOAN: Or "I want to get something out of this. This is going to do something for me."

TONI: Does one get caught up in this desire to get something out of it, which involves imagining how much better off I would be if I had this compared to the way I am now? Can one see comparison operating? Trying is a palpable engagement; it has physical manifestations. The body faithfully responds to every thought, to every desire projected in the mind.

So either there is entanglement in this project—thought wanting to get something out of quiet listening, becoming a better person—or one

sees the caught-up-ness. If there is no seeing, then there will be trying—trying to find a method, the right person to train with, and whatever else goes with this trying we've been doing for hundreds of years.

JOAN: You talk a lot about our tendency to always look for authorities outside of ourselves. I notice that there's something scary about not
having an authority, because I really don't know what I am or why I'm
here. I don't really know *anything*, that's the bottom line. So I find myself reaching for somebody who does know.

TONI: What is it that you want from somebody you call an authority? And what is scary about standing alone?

JOAN: I think what I want is security, almost a kind of parental feeling—somebody who knows.

TONI: And someone who will tell you what to do? Or how life is?

JOAN: Yes. What I should be doing, that everything is okay, and that
there's a program I can follow that makes sense. Otherwise thought
says maybe life is totally meaningless, maybe I'm all alone in a huge,
unfriendly void. Maybe there's no program, there's nothing to do.

TONI: What's scary about that—no program and nothing to do?

[*Toni and Joan both laugh.*]

JOAN: I see myself caught up in seemingly destructive patterns of behavior, like compulsively biting my fingers, and I want help getting out of
those patterns. I want to be freed. And I want some certainty that everything is fundamentally okay, that I'm not all alone in a meaningless void.

TONI: Does it help if somebody says to you, "Don't fear, I will guide
you. I'll tell you that life is meaningful. I'll give you a meditation practice"? Is that helpful? Seeing what goes on in the mind—the repetitive
patterns, the mechanicalness, the meaninglessness of it—what is scary
about *seeing* it? Does scariness come in when thought says, "Oh my
God, is that all I am? I need somebody to guide me into something
other than these thought patterns"?

Who can reveal to you what is going on in this mind? We can talk
and write about it, but then it's more ideas about the separate "me," it's
thoughts with their elating or depressive orchestration. But directly
perceiving thoughts and their quick links to emotion—that can only
happen in yourself. No one can do that for you.

JOAN: My experience is that it has been helpful to encounter other people like you who seem to see clearly. But then I begin to latch on to other people's words in a way that has to do with wanting security or answers. And that isn't helpful. I can see myself do it in a moment of anxiety. I may reach for a spiritual book, for example.

TONI: All right, let's take that. In a moment of anxiety you reach for a spiritual book. What happens? Have you observed it, given some careful attention to it? The anxiety is what?

JOAN: It's thought.

TONI: Just thought?

JOAN: It's thought and whatever thought triggers in the way of sensations in the body, emotions.

TONI: And why is it so hard to be with these emotions and see the connections to the thoughts that have triggered them? Is it that these emotions trigger resistance—"I don't want to feel this way"—fear of the feeling?

JOAN: I suspect it goes far back into infancy or even fetal life—the initial, primal experiences of separation and otherness. It triggers something very old, something deeply conditioned.

TONI: But however deeply conditioned and far back in time it may go, it is happening *now*.

JOAN: Yes.

TONI: There is the thought, then the sensations, then the resistance or fear of feeling the fear. And out of this whole mass of happenings comes reaching for a book to escape. Is that it?

JOAN: Yes.

TONI: Now what happens when you read a passage in the book?

JOAN: When I do it in that spirit, it's very unsatisfying. I can feel how I'm desperately looking for something, and it's never there.

TONI: What are you looking for?

JOAN: A feeling of being completely at peace, no longer wanting or fearing or feeling separate from anything. But reading a book that way is like the old saying about reading the menu instead of eating the meal. It's words describing something that has to be done or gone into. The real task is to put the book down and just be with the anxiety, the sensations. But maybe that becomes an idea, too: I *should* put the book down and be with the anxiety. Behind it all is this picture of a "me" who is trying to steer my way toward a state of being where I'm finally at peace.

TONI: And what's at the root of this sense of a self that doesn't want to feel the way it's feeling right now and wants to steer itself into a better way with the help of authority or books or techniques? What is that, that sense of "me the suffering one" or "me the liberated one" and *my* path to that liberation? What is all of that?

JOAN: It seems that "me" is only there if there is thinking. There has to be some thought like "This feeling is happening to me, and I don't like it. I could be feeling better, and there must be a way to get to a better state." It's all thinking. It's all imagination, isn't it?

TONI: Is it? Do you *see* it? Do you see it together with the sound of the birds, the breeze?

In this listening space of birdsong, breathing, sunshine the idea arises: "I am perceiving all of this." With that thought, the "me" is instantly reborn, and with it a host of associated ideas and images and longings. Can the openness happen without identifying with *any* of the thoughts?

JOAN: It can, but it seems that thought tends to turn everything into an object or a concept. When openness occurs, thought comes in and forms an *idea* of it: this is "openness," and I want to keep it or get it back or have it forever.

TONI: And what prevents you from perceiving *that*, and *this*, and *this* and *this*—what is arising, what has just ceased—from moment to moment? So that whatever happens, whether it's an opening or a closing, it's just what it is. It need not be tackled or dealt with. Nothing need be done about it, for or against it.

JOAN: Toni, I've wondered a lot about how change happens. I've gone through a number of major changes in my life—giving up heavy drinking and smoking, for example. And then there are other habits that I have not been successful at giving up, like obsessively thinking about the future. At the time I quit drinking, I thought I knew how it happened. I had a model for it. But looking back on it, I'm not really sure what happened. I wonder, do we have a choice about changing our behavior? Is there a self that has the ability to stand back and observe itself and decide that a certain behavior should be changed and then make that change?

TONI: Maybe the best way of approaching such a complex question is simply to start from scratch, not asking how does one change, but rather looking at what we mean by change. We assume that words we use a lot are understood; whereas in looking more closely we realize that we're using language very mechanically. What do we mean by change?

JOAN: It seems that it relies a lot on thought and memory, on the memory of how I used to be, on the idea of how I am now, and then the projected, imagined idea of how I could be.

TONI: Yes. To talk about change we need mental processes like comparison and memory. If there were no memory or comparison, there would just be what is going on right now, not in comparison to what was a moment ago or ten years ago, but just what's going on now. There would be no possibility of talking about change. If there were no projection of imagination into the future—what I could be or will be—then there would not be any thought of change. There would just be living this moment as it is, not comparing now to how it was or how it could be. Future and past are mental operations of thought and memory.

So how can I change? This question has permeated our conversation. How can I be free from conditioned patterns? How can I become an enlightened person, not caught up in thoughts or fear or anger?

Aren't we trying to change something that we don't even understand in depth? We *think* we know what we are because we can talk about it, but are we really in touch with ourselves from moment to moment—the angry moments, the fearful moments, the hopeful moments, the trying moments? What *is* all of that *directly*? Isn't that approach different from cataloguing ourselves—I'm angry, I'm addicted, I'm fearful, I'm suffering, I would like to change into some other state—going from catalog to catalog?

JOAN: Judging comes in so quickly. I'm doing something like uncontrollably biting my fingers, and there's a judgment that this is not good, and also a real experience that it's hurtful. And there may be the memory of times when it wasn't going on when I felt better. So I want to get rid of it. And you're saying, look at what it is.

TONI: Really look. Watch patiently—not just taking a glimpse and then immediately evaluating, "Nothing has changed. The looking is no good. I have to have a different method, but really *being* with biting your fingers. *What is that?* Give it the attention and care and time and patience and interest that you would give your dearest friend. So what is this biting? How does it happen? How does it feel? Not "I want to be rid of it," because the moment you want to be rid of something, thought is going on, and thought prevents immediacy.

JOAN: It seems to create a separation, too. There's "me," and then there's this thing that I'm being afflicted with. I can imagine myself being happier if this thing weren't there.

TONI: And that *is* the feeling of separation. That is the separate "me" that should be different. But at a moment of feeling the actual sensations of the finger between the teeth, all of that, there's no "me" in that. There is just what *is* going on. What is going on? Let go of the thought of change. It goes away by itself when there is the intensity of being here with what is happening.

JOAN: When you say just being here with what is happening, you don't mean in an analytical way. You don't mean thinking back to when did this habit start, and is it due to this or that. You mean being with the physical sensations, hearing the thoughts that are popping up as it's happening, right?

TONI: Yes, and the throbbing heart, the movement of breath, the tightness in the chest. And one is not falling into thinking that this is bad. *Not feeling down on oneself.* When this open listening happens, thought does not intrude, because thought is not needed. The immediacy of being needs no thought.

One could pause for a moment with the itch to bite, maybe just watching the very first impulse to do that. Caring attention interrupts the mechanical pattern. The desire to bite the fingers has been a mechanical accompaniment to all kinds of thoughts, memories, and feelings, and one has never really felt that desire before. At this moment of being here, it's new. It's transparent what happens with desire—wanting something, imagining oneself having what one wants: freedom, peace, security, enlightenment. And at the same time, there is the fear of not getting what one desires. The whole body system plays its accompaniment—grasping, tensing, biting mechanically. Now it's all revealed without judgment. Is *this* the change—completely being here without being anything?

JOAN: Toni, your way of working is very open. Here at Springwater there are no precepts for how one ought to behave. There are forms at any given moment—we hold retreats in complete silence—but none of these forms are considered a sacred tradition. They're always open to question and to being changed. People are not required during retreats to come to sittings or talks. If a person wants to spend the entire retreat in bed, that is perfectly okay. In looking as we have been at how to work with what's going on in one's life, what you're suggesting is not to adopt a method or a program or to try to take control or use will, but rather to simply be alive from moment to moment, and to question *any* agenda that thought begins to construct. Sometimes that seems scary to me. I'm afraid sloth and torpor and addictive habits will take over. Why are you working in this open, unstructured way?

TONI: I don't think I can come up with any reason. I cannot do otherwise. I'm not choosing from a bunch of options and trying to decide which is the best way. This is a choiceless way.

JOAN: In other words, it's just what's happening.

TONI: Yes.

JOAN: And you don't know where it's going.

TONI: How could we know where it's going? Thought can project, but that is again stepping out of the immediacy of being here and into speculation. That process of speculation can come into awareness. And whatever awareness touches . . . something changes. A pattern gives way to awareness. The energy of the habitual pattern is now the energy of awareness.

JOAN: Do you see a problem with a more intentional or directed approach? If I decide I believe in nonviolence and take a vow not to kill, do you see a problem with that?

TONI: Well, flashing back over our centuries-old fascination with vows and precepts, it seems they haven't done us much good. We have a history of transgressing precepts. I think it is for each one of us to observe whether deciding to do something helps to throw light on how we actually are. Does resolving to be nonviolent throw light on our violence? If it does, then what is important is the light, the attention and care that is given to this present violent thought or reaction.

If you say that awareness of violence could have happened only because you took a vow, I would keep watching and questioning whether awareness is caused by anything. At the moment of a violent outbreak of hatred in oneself, is there attention? Or is there suppression because one remembers the vow? Suppression does not help to clarify and bring about change. Change *is* awareness of habitual, mechanical movement.

So find out for yourself. Does vow taking result in suppression—not wanting to face the condemned response of violence—or does it shed light? Unless something is allowed to reveal itself openly, there cannot be change. Patterns of suppression continue.

JOAN: One thing that seems to be emphasized here at Springwater is looking into the images we have about ourselves and other people, and a process of meeting each other—looking not just at our different opinions and ideas, but also at the way we *identify* with those opinions and ideas and feel as if our life is being threatened if someone disagrees with us. Could you talk some about the importance of working with other people?

TONI: Even if you are only interested in finding out what is happening in yourself, without the challenge of relationship, how will you find out? If you isolate yourself, a lot of buttons will not be pushed. It's only in relationship that our deep-seated programs of defense, attack, and hurt are mobilized. We mirror and trigger each other. What is hurt in myself is also hurt in you. You say something that hurts the image that I have of myself, and I say something back that hurts your image of yourself. If that is all that is going on, then nothing is learned. Something else has to enter into the relationship: open, spacious listening to what is going on in myself as you talk, as I am about to attack you or defend myself. Without this new element of open listening, we will just keep on going in our habitual patterns. The patterns may change, but the mechanical nature of our responses will continue.

JOAN: Suppose somebody says something to me that is racist or sexist or hurtful to a whole group of people, maybe a group I'm a part of. I hear what is said, and I feel the blood rush to my head. How would you work with that?

TONI: Can we draw each other's attention, see that blood is rushing to the head, and wonder what is going on? Can we also draw each other's attention to the fact that a racist remark has just been made, so that we all become aware of what is going on in ourselves and in each other?

And what is a racist remark? Where is it coming from? Our conditioning is to say it's coming from the other person—you are racist. As though you or I were voluntarily, freely engaged in this thing called racism. But maybe it's not a voluntary and spontaneous engagement. Maybe what is discovered upon careful looking, alone and together, is that what is manifesting are collective patterns that have existed in human society for centuries.

So how am I going to meet a racist remark? What will be my response? That I've got to tackle it, change it, get rid of it, teach you not to do that, keep the blood from rushing to my head, or I've got to express my indignation? These are all the doings. They are age-old and habitual and have no insight, no space. Or will there be space to see racism come up in oneself or another person, without judgment, and therefore the freedom to see what it does, how it separates, and how judgment, justification, or condemnation does not reveal it in its fullness? The full revelation, the fullness of attention, is the change.

Can we help each other by looking at what's there, discovering the resistance, the judgment of each other and ourselves? Can we help each other create a space in which *everything* can be seen, felt, heard, and experienced as it is, as it is coming up?

Is that what is lacking in our collective efforts to change and better ourselves and the world? We are forever coming up with new ideas and programs, but what's lacking is the space, the quietness and care of attending to our problems, allowing them to reveal themselves and to be seen spaciously. They reveal themselves as not just my problem or your problem, but a common problem. If we were to meet each other like that, wouldn't a new relationship unfold among us? Wouldn't a shared attention unfold, a shared care for what's there in us—the racism, the anger, the violence, the resistance, the desire to be better?

JOAN: There is something healing about listening and the spaciousness around listening.

TONI: What do you mean by healing?

JOAN: When I'm in the presence of someone else who is listening openly to me, it allows me to listen openly myself. When there is listening and space, there isn't any problem anymore.

TONI: So what about the racist remark that someone just made?

JOAN: It's not that racism or sexism shouldn't be corrected. But the *problem* aspect has to do with what makes the blood rush to the head. The problem has to do with the sense that somebody is *deliberately* doing this to *me* to hurt *me*, instead of seeing that it's all a conditioned pattern that we're all caught up in, a pattern of ideas and thoughts manifesting in the whole social fabric.

TONI: Including the conditioned pattern that there is an "I" who does things deliberately and a "me" who is a victim of that deliberate doing of the other. That itself is patterned thinking.

JOAN: Right. So when I say that the problem is gone, I don't mean that discrimination or prejudice is okay. I mean that the charge of feeling personally victimized by people who are out to get *me* disappears.

TONI: And maybe without that feeling reaction, there is a creative energy that allows one to express something clearly, without revenge or attack or self-defense.

JOAN: Our habitual ways of trying to correct social problems often separate us again when we act out of self-righteous anger.

TONI: Yes, because such responses nurture this feeling of "me" and "you" as separate, different, irreconcilable. There's also the pleasure of attacking, of having a position—it's all there to wonder about.

JOAN: Would you say that the feeling of separation between us only comes up when thought is going on? In some sense there *is* "me" and "you"—two independent organisms with different experiences and interests.

TONI: I wonder whether the deer on this land feel separate or together or whether all of this is just a product of thinking/feeling. The processes that are involved in thinking, "I'm a Jew, and you're a Palestinian"—these processes of attachment and identification with the image of "me," whatever it may exclude or include, and the feeling of togetherness and separateness that we experience because of our identifications—these are all made possible by this immense brain we have. Even though one may identify with one group and someone else with a different group, identification is the same for all of us, and it makes for a physically sensed feeling of separation. Insight can reveal and dissipate completely the feeling of separation. At the moment of insight, the system of separatist thinking is quiet. The energy is in listening openly.

JOAN: Toni, one last question. Sometimes people say to me that this work is just a head trip. It's not going to do anything about the problems of the world. It's perceived to be very mental, not connected to life as a whole, to the body or the feelings.

TONI: Doesn't it depend on how we are listening? If we are listening just mentally, then, of course, whatever is said is mental, or it is perceived that way. As the listening deepens, it includes the totality of this organism, every fiber and pore listening, not divided into head or body. What's the difference between head and body? It's all one organism inseparably interrelated with this whole universe. Isn't it? In such open, wholesome listening, there is nothing "heady." It is all of oneself, and at the same time nothing at all.

Nothing Spectacular

There is the wind, the sound of rustling leaves, the brightness of the room, the breathing, the color of the wooden floor, the hands resting, the heart beating. There is saliva gathering in the mouth, and the swallowing of it. What's so hard about being in touch with what is real, with what is *actually* here this moment, unspectacular though it may be?

Is this one of our problems? That to be in touch with reality we expect something spectacular, something out of the ordinary? So we fail to be with our feet on the most ordinary of grounds, a soggy path or a wooden floor, a rug.

Last night in the meeting room there was a lamp on the table, and just beneath it a small plant with the greenest of leaves, like tongues unfolding out of the little pot, and a few red flowers, as red as red can be, with yellow dots inside. That simple. Can we see it and not expect this to do something for us? Can we just see it, hear it, feel it completely?

At the same time there is the breathing, the sound of the wind, the ticking of a clock, and the beating of the heart. A feeling of uncertainty or calm may also be there. The entire universe is there—the wonder of it, not the concept. Just the air, the ground, the sky, the night, the stars, and the lights of Springwater.

This chapter was adapted from a retreat talk delivered in February 1990.

How Is One to Look?

In being here quietly, attentively, not escaping, not resisting, but really seeing the whole thing through from beginning to end, there is no danger at all. It is true being.

The brain is constantly active. In the midst of the barrage of remembrances, associations, feelings, reactions, judgments, impulses—this whole ongoing Niagara of consciousness—how is one to look?

Not long ago on a Sunday afternoon, a mother with a seven-month-old baby came to visit Springwater. People just naturally gathered around. The baby was watching everything. He was not in that state of self-consciousness "Look at me!" or "Watch me!" That wasn't there.

After feeding the baby, the mother put him down on the floor, and he started scratching the rug back and forth. Having put away food jars, spoon, and bib, the mother took a brightly colored musical ball out of her bag and rolled it toward the baby. The baby instantly stopped scratching the rug and focused on the ball, pushing it, watching it, listening to it—all of him right there with all of it.

Someone entered through the door. The baby looked up. In the total movement of his tiny body turning toward the door, the eyes watching the new person, there was simple attention. No "effort" was made to be attentive. A baby doesn't make an effort to be attentive. It just happens.

Years later we suddenly ask, "How are we to look?" For almost all of us, there was such a time when feeling, touching, listening, hearing, and seeing were all one movement in harmony with the environment, not separate from it. The moving of a tree in the wind was the moving of the head, the body, the eyes looking, the ears listening.

This chapter was adapted from a talk given during the retreat of June 1990 and was published in the Springwater Center Newsletter *of October 1990.*

While the baby was rolling the colored ball, someone put a football near him. He immediately reached out to touch it. The mother appeared concerned—the football was a bit dirty, so she picked it up and put it aside. The baby flopped forward on his hands, knees, and belly, crawling toward it. Did he already want it because it had been taken away from him?

The football certainly wasn't as colorful and as noisy as the bright plastic ball, but he'd already played with that, and this was something new. But the mother kept the football out of his reach, and he didn't fuss. There were lots of other things to investigate. Later on, the football was within close reach, the mother wasn't looking, and the baby was licking it. Not just touching it, but licking it. All the senses were there in one exploring. Not because he had a meditation "practice"!

Do we have one? Many of us have a meditation practice. Is the conditioning to practice in a certain way a hindrance to attending openly, freely, to what is going on within and around us?

How is one to look? Is there a "how"? Or is there just looking—a moment of waking up from thought and fantasy, and simply realizing what is going on? Seeing at a glance what thought and feelings are occupied with? And what is going on besides the fantasy right this moment—the sounds all around, breathing, feeling the warmth of the air and the coolness of the breeze, a moment of *just this*, without the intention to look or listen. One is not caught by the thought "I must pay attention" or "I must keep this practice going."

So this is our question: at the moment of waking up from thought and fantasy, what is there? Not immediately getting lost in a new train of thought "What should I do now?" or "How should I look?" one is watching what is actually happening right now. It doesn't have to be verbalized.

It's not "How should I look?" but what is happening when there is an instant of simple looking and listening?

Does the brain immediately bring up instructions on how to proceed? Then the openness is gone—replaced by the narrowness of conforming to instructions, or the confusion about what instructions to follow. Can that be seen directly as it happens? The amazing thing is that the awakened mind has the capacity to see at a glance not only that a dream has taken place but also the whole content of it—the desires, the fears, the pleasures and pains of past and future.

The dream may have evoked pleasant or unpleasant feelings throughout the body. They need not become cause for conflict. They're just there right now. Of course, when they are pleasant, we don't consider them a problem. But if we want to continue with pleasure, *that* becomes a problem. When there is anxiety or pain we make a problem out of it. We make problems out of everything! Why? Can we just be with *what is*?

Being unconditionally alone with fear or pain is something we dread, because we may never have done it before. It's something that seems dangerous, and we think it will bring more pain: pain without end. All kinds of false assumptions exist in the brain about the danger of directly facing fear or pain.

In being here quietly, attentively, not escaping, not resisting, but really seeing the whole thing through from beginning to end, there is no danger at all. It is true being. The "pain," the "anxiety," is not what thought says it is. It can be felt, lived with directly. It can be survived. Not just survived, but transparently understood. Fear ends in this moment of no–separation.

Direct seeing is the light of discovery. A new energy is operating. Energy is released when there is no escape, no resistance, no will, no opposition, no division between "me" and "my pain"—no thing!

How does one look at a flower? Does the brain immediately scan the memory to find the right name? And what about all the comments about it and the reactions: "I like it" or "I don't like it"? Where is the real flower, the whole flower?

Recently some of us were hiking in the mountains through carpets of flowers. One person wondered if the tiny blossoms close to the ground were fragrant. It took quite a while of pondering in the abstract before someone actually knelt down and took a sniff.

Can the word "flower" be seen for what it is—a name, a label, with many associations that usually interfere with direct perception? We can experiment with this if we're interested. We have seen so many flowers and "know" them from memory. We see the remembrance instead of the real thing right in front of our eyes. We may have drawn and painted them, photographed them, or made arrangements of them. All that stuff enters into the looking and obscures clarity.

What happens in looking at just one flower? Can the word "flower" be put aside, so one looks afresh, like a little baby not knowing it's a flower but seeing something strikingly yellow and red, going to it, touching it, pulling at it? I'm not advocating that we pull flowers, although our son used to do that as a toddler. He even ate flowers. Particularly begonias. Little fibrous begonias. He would pick one after another and eat them.

If one wonders like a little baby what this thing is, then what is it? How does one look? Can there be a looking without the "me"? Just looking. Not "forever" or "for a long time" or "longer than last time," but looking. Not knowing what it is, or what it will bring. Not knowing what "looking" is or what the flower is. *Just this.*

Yearning for Completion

The thought of "me" is of necessity incomplete.

When the sense of "me" is present with its deep feelings of insufficiency and incompleteness, with its endless searching for perfection and security, we can't see freely. There is always that feeling of incompleteness as I think about myself.

The thought of "me" is of necessity incomplete. Any thought is incomplete. There is no complete thought. Thought comes from fragmented memories that can never ever capture the aliveness of this moment. No matter how much I think about myself, what I am, how I am, what I should be—it's never the whole live thing, because I am immeasurably more than the fragmented thoughts and pictures and feelings about myself.

Thought and feeling cannot be complete. The completeness of life cannot be captured in thought or feeling. Thought is trying to do it all the time, but it can't. We live in thoughts and feelings, alone and with others who are conditioned in the same way.

From the thought-feeling of incompleteness arises wanting and fearing. Wanting completion and fearing the absence of it. Wanting fulfillment, meaning, and purpose. Wanting and fearing. In observing carefully, one finds that not a moment goes by without some wanting or fearing. Even if there is a moment of fulfillment, there comes the desire for more of it or the fear that this moment will end. One wants to keep it, wants to prolong it. All of it comes out of this feeling of incompleteness, which inevitably goes with the idea of "me" as a separate entity.

This chapter was adapted from a retreat talk given in February 1990 and was published in the Springwater Center Newsletter *of July 1994.*

And then there is the trying. Trying to become complete. Trying to become complete through thought: the spiritual paths, the exercises, the imposed practices, whether self-imposed or imposed by a discipline that one takes up, trying to become complete through time. It is all thought. Do we see that? Both the incompleteness we suffer from and the completeness we strive toward are thoughts and images.

It is all an escape from what is actually happening right now, this very instant—simple all-encompassing presence without lack, un-thinkable, vast, indivisible.

Grieving

Not wanting to feel the ache of loss, one may strain at various practices in the hope of "staying in the present," struggling to transcend the grieving process.

Dear Toni,

It is nice to be writing to you again after what seems like many years and no time at all. This has been a year of great change for me, and certain questions have arisen for me that I am struggling with. I would like your perspective.

Many years ago, in a talk, you made a statement that I have never forgotten. You spoke of your receiving news that your father had died. You said that your very first reaction was to feel yourself choking, perhaps with the grief or shock, and then you experienced the realization that the father you remembered was of the past, not the present. As soon as there was just this presence, there was nothing to grieve. I may have changed the words about some, but that is the gist of what you offered to us that day. Now, years later, when it is much more meaningful to me in terms of my own experience, I'd like to ask you about this.

At the beginning of this year my closest friend, my sister, took her life. Despite knowing that she, indeed, was beyond all her suffering and pain, for me the pain was terrible. And it was for my mother, too. In April my mother, unable to find peace with this event, suffered a heart attack and stroke, and after two weeks she died. I spent every day with her during that time, and after she died I began the long and tedious work of settling her estate. Being busy was a help, and in July I went west to Colorado, rented a cabin near Longs Peak, and began to

---

This chapter contains Toni's reponse to a November 1991 letter from a friend. It was published in the Springwater Center Newsletter *of July 1992.*

really feel and experience my own grief. It was during this time that I thought a great deal about what you had said in that talk and wondered for whom such an instant course of recovery would be possible. I give you credit for having seen through illusion in the deepest way, and I accept that perhaps you can thus transcend the sorrow that humanity experiences regarding loss. But my conclusion has been that grief is a tricky and dangerous thing, and that one must be extraordinarily careful not to repress it in the hope of staying in the present and transcending the whole process. I do believe that there is no suffering in the present, in the instant of now, but I also believe that grieving is a process that loss entails, and we skip it at our peril.

Yet it appears to me that you might not really be saying to skip the grieving process, as it seemed you did regarding your father. It would appear that in the whole process of exploring and feeling fully every aspect of one's humanness, one could simply sit with the terrible pain and question it in the deepest sense, going through it to a place where it is no longer the *pain* of loss, but an *understanding* of loss. I have not done this. But I have watched how the pain works. When something comes along to remind me of my sister or my mother, my heart has constricted with pain, and I recognize that "past" events trigger the pain. And every book or article or "expert" on death and dying that I have read encourages the grieving process, the flow of tears that remembering brings. The tears themselves are a cleansing, a form of healing I find. Do you follow my confusion here? Part of me would love to leapfrog the whole grieving process, to be so in and aware of the present that no suffering or "loss" would be experienced. And part of me warns that time and again I will be reminded of the loss and must feel the pain, but that I can let it go, allow it to flow through me, not hold onto it. Perhaps it is the holding on that is dangerous.

I am sure you have addressed this issue many times, but not in the books I have. I need to know if you think all of us can handle sudden death, or any death as you did your father's, or if you think we need to be with the grief. The answers seem obvious in that we need to do what comes up for us individually. I remember I wanted to ask you whether if Kyle died, after so long and close a relationship, if you think you would respond as you did to your father's death. Perhaps the closeness would evoke a different response, and, of course, one can't know until that time.

Well, old friend, I am finding my way. Your input will be so very welcome. Reduced to simple terms I am asking if you would not agree that for most of us grieving is a necessary stage, but one that can be seen through with deep silence and inner questioning.

Dear ———,

I was saddened to hear about the traumatic losses of both your dear sister and your mother in such a short period of time. And yet there was the joy of hearing from you again after so many years.

Just the day before receiving your letter Kyle and I were attending a gathering in memory of a dear friend who had died from lung cancer. A small circle of relatives and friends were standing close together amidst the moist fragrance of brightly colored chrysanthemums and the soft sound of dripping water in a spacious greenhouse. We heard from the son and the husband about our friend's last months, weeks, and hours, spent in much equanimity and beauty. She died holding both sons' hands with a faint smile on her face. Apparently she had never been in real pain—at least she did not mention it or give evidence of it; she just had increasing difficulty with breathing. Maybe the beauty and equanimity was that of letting go. When her husband was asked whether he felt she was holding on, he replied, "No, she wasn't, but we were."

Let us look carefully at what you write in your letter. Can we put aside all the ideas and conclusions we have gathered in the past about death, grieving, and healing and start wondering and looking afresh right now?

One's mother, sister, wife, father, brother, husband, or dearest friend has died. They are no longer here. They are gone. That is so. Is it dangerous to see clearly that everything coming up in the mindbody about the deceased is a remembrance, and that the intense pain, the constriction of the heart, the pressure in the chest, the flooding of the eyes—the grief and sense of loss taking place this very instant—that it is all connected with vivid reminders of what was, and what, theoretically, still could be?

This insight may or may not disperse pain and grief this moment. It's clear that memory images can arise at any moment, triggered by almost anything reminiscent of the lost one, and that with these reminders may come the intense pain and agony of grief. But again, can there be anything tricky and dangerous in clearly seeing that this is actually happening? Being fully aware of whatever is taking place this instant needs nothing else. Open awareness has its own unfathomable wisdom and right action.

What is truly dangerous, as you yourself write, is to think that one has seen through all this while one is actually repressing pain and grief. Not wanting to feel the ache of loss, one may strain at various practices in the hope of "staying in the present," struggling to transcend the grieving process. Repression is the escaping from what is, without any real understanding: in this case, not wanting to experience pain, denying feelings of loss, or trying to live up to heroic images of being the transcender of sorrow. Repression does not play a part in seeing into the whole ongoing process of grieving.

It can be seen directly and experienced clearly that any memory of a beloved friend or relative who died can instantly arouse mental and physical pain, grief, anguish, and maybe guilt. The memories of intimate, joyful times, of shared concerns, of difficulties lived through together, and things the two of us didn't do together and could still have done together—the vividness with which all of this appears instantly on the internal memory screen, and then again the shattering realization that all of this is irretrievably gone forever, never to be had again—it can turn the entire mindbody into a flood of heartache, tears, and depression.

And grief may not be aroused just by thoughts and imagery. If we have lived together closely and shared much energy together, having become dependent on giving and receiving energy, then the breaking up of this shared energy field leaves an aching wound, probably not unlike the loss of part of one's own body.

Awareness also may reveal that the mindbody wants to repeat over and over again the same remembrances, to go along the same trains of thought, to feel the same feelings. It is as though we cannot or do not want to be done with all of that. We become addicted to our own mental grooves. There also may be the confusion of contradictory thought-commands such as "I need to fully experience all of my grief in order to heal" and "I must transcend grief in order to be free."

You write, "[It] appears to me that you might not really be saying to skip the grieving process, . . . [but] that in the whole process of exploring and feeling fully every aspect of our humanness, one could simply sit with the terrible pain and question it in the deepest sense, going through it to a place where it is no longer the *pain* of loss, but an *understanding* of loss." Yes, that puts it well.

Can we directly see and experience how strongly our whole system is influenced by ideas like "I ought to overcome the pain of grief" or "I must encourage the grieving process like all the experts recommend"? Is it clear that a mind beset with ideas and choices cannot be open to experiencing something spontaneously right now? Can having ideas give way to letting unfold gently, without strain, what is actually happening now? We don't know what to do about it all, but do we have to? Not knowing what will be next, can we attend carefully to what is taking place this instant?

I do not know whether we must grieve or not, and whether we can live healthily without it. I really don't know. I don't encourage others or myself to do this or that, and I don't discourage anything either. Either encouragement or discouragement would override the direct discovery of what is actually unfolding right now. And that is what I'm passionately interested in—coming directly upon what is true right now, being completely open without knowing. Do you see what I mean?

I do not know if any of us can really "handle" sudden or lingering death, or if we need to be able to do so. Death has its own unfathomable wake. We know nothing about it.

I also don't know if I would respond to my husband's death in the way I did to my father's passing. Most likely not, because ours is such a different relationship, the tremendous closeness of it, the long years we've spent living and sharing so intimately together. I don't really know. I'll see when it happens, if I'm alive to see it.

I'm not afraid to think of death, mine or Kyle's, nor anyone else's, but thinking about death isn't dying. Thinking cannot know dying. Dying is the ending of trying to figure things out, the ending of thinking and knowing. There is no place to go, nothing to fear or seek, no one and nothing to hold on to, nothing to continue.

Dying right now is the utter transparency and ceasing of memory images and emotions in the present aliveness of what is. There may still be leftover sensations from memories throbbing throughout body, but these are not separate from the sound of wind howling in the eaves and trees, snowflakes dancing, birds singing, breath flowing, heart beating in this vast, silent space of nothing at all—no thought about myself as past, present, or future. There is no desire to be or not to be, to endure, to keep, or to transcend. There is no fear of ending. Just what is, without needing to know.

Healing is the ending of separation.

Fear of Silence

Let's just stay with the fear, the scariness, of not being here as solid "me," of being no one, of having no future. . . . What comes up?

One moment of complete aliveness without any word. Without division into "me" and "that." It cannot be described, cannot be put into words. What about the fear that may come up so quickly, the fear of silence? Why does fear of silence arise? What is it?

A moment of being here without that solid sense of "me" may quickly turn into a threat the moment *thinking about it* arises. Sometimes it feels like the fear of dying, sometimes the fear of losing all that one holds dear, all that one is attached to or invested in. A warning light seems to start revolving in the brain, saying, "Watch out! Don't go further! This is dangerous ground!" Dangerous to what? To whom?

Am I jumping ahead? Let's just stay with the fear, the scariness, of not being here as solid "me," of being no one, of having no future. . . . What comes up? Will we immediately be caught up in the content of these thoughts and the sensations and emotions that arise throughout the body? Imagined danger triggers the same responses as real danger, doesn't it? Can there be a pause in this vast stream of conditioned thinking and reacting—a quiet inward looking and listening without knowing, a pause that may disengage the momentum of the past while shedding light on it?

Why do we trust our fantasy of what will be there if there is no holding on to this thought/image of "me"? "I'll be a dehumanized robot," we may think. But actually isn't that what we are *now*, with all

---

This chapter was adapted from a retreat talk and published in the Springwater Center Newsletter *of April 1993.*

this "me-ness" and identification? Aren't we forever reacting automatically, protecting and defending something, but hurting nonetheless?

So when there's a moment of no sense of "me," why not leave it alone completely, come what may? When a fearful thought or feeling arises in an instant, it can also be gone in an instant, even before it has triggered the thirty thousand chemicals throughout the body. There is just a vulnerable being exposed, alone, without knowing, without a word. Maybe it's a moment of dying to all the impulses to know, to protect, to maintain, to continue. Not knowing is dying. And at the same time being wholly alive.

Images in Relationship

We think *we are responding to each other consciously,*
spontaneously, out of the present situation, but we're not.
Instead, stored-up images and programs, with their connected
feelings and emotions, are constantly being triggered and
projected.

In many human beings there is a deep fear of relationship, of being rejected, hurt, or misunderstood. We may avoid relationship yet long for it, because human beings are born into relationship, for better or worse. And we are born out of relationship. We wouldn't be here if there hadn't been a relationship between our parents. There is a great yearning in human beings for companionship, for being together, for sharing.

Little children gravitate toward each other, play together, or often just watch each other. When they are being pushed in shopping carts in a supermarket, they will find each other with their eyes and watch each other with consuming interest.

A man who had been coming to the Springwater Center for many years spent a vacation in a remote place in the Canadian Rockies to hike alone over mountain ranges, glaciers, and streams. He had arranged to be dropped off by plane and to be met again after six weeks of solitary wandering. He wanted to find out what it is like to be really alone. Alone in the wilderness, on his way back to the plane's pickup place, he saw a tiny figure in the distance, which he knew must be a human being. Immediately he noticed his drained energies picking up. He began walking more briskly, then running, and, upon meeting this stranger, he embraced him. He didn't know who the man was; he had never seen him before. It wasn't that he wanted anything of that person, he just hugged him because he was there.

This chapter was adapted from a retreat talk given May 1989 and was published in the Springwater Center Newsletter *of October 1993.*

There is a great yearning in us for love and companionship. Yet our relationships cause immense conflicts, violence, and heartaches. Why? Why does the joy of just being together on a walk, sharing a meal, playing together, or having sex so quickly turn into something else? Can we examine this? We first have to understand where our yearning for companionship comes from.

Is the fear of being lonely, of being unloved, the driving force for seeking companionship? Are we seeking someone to fill the aching inner emptiness?

What about insecurity? Not being sure of myself, feeling negative about myself, I want somebody to tell me that I'm attractive and lovable. When someone says those things to me, the chemicals get going. I feel alive. I long to be with this person so that I'll continue to feel good about myself. The one who makes me feel this way appears in glowing images in my mind. When I'm with him or her, I don't see the actual person. I see him or her through the image of the ideal companion who makes me feel alive. Not only do I love the verbal flattery, but I also love the way he or she approaches, looking at me with adoring or longing eyes. I adore myself through this person.

I remember experiencing this in my teens in World War II Germany. It was after I developed my first real crush on a young soldier who was home on leave. There weren't many young men around then because they were in the war. Just a few came home on leave occasionally, maybe for a week or two. So mostly they weren't around. And I felt a tremendous yearning to be with a young man.

Finally I met one, but he was already on his last day of furlough, and then he'd be off to the front again. He wrote letters. How I read and reread those letters to bathe in the magic words about myself: that I was beautiful, that he loved me, and how much he missed me. I was much more concerned with myself than I was with this young man, but that wasn't clear to me at the time. If you had asked me then, I would have said that I was in love with *him*. But I was in love with *myself*. I was looking for *me* in his letters.

And there never seemed to be enough of them either. There was always the need for more, because chemicals come and go; eventually they get flushed out. One needs new stimulation, a new rush from more affirmation, more words, more touch.

We human beings do this to each other at the time of courting. We're at our best then, saying to the other what we sense he or she wants to hear. We're like a bird displaying his brightest feathers, or a bullfrog croaking his finest song. But for the animals, when the mating season is over, the courting rituals end. Animals go back to "normal." Not so with human beings. For us the season goes on.

Being on our best behavior, though, is hard to keep up. We are projecting our own image onto the other person, and then we are relating to the image we have created of the other person. Then if two people start living together, in the nitty-gritty of daily life, things change somehow. For one thing, we find out more about each other's habits and rigidities. We also discover that flirting and courting behavior isn't the basis for a continuing relationship. And getting used to each other, we may find the present relationship boring and start flirting with someone else.

When the courtship wears off and we're with each other day in and day out, the partner may increasingly trigger the memory, the image of someone else—the father or the mother, the stereotyped male or female, the dominant one who always gets his or her own way. Projections arise from our memories of past relationships, and what happens in the present relationship is interpreted according to our earlier experiences. Whatever we have done to each other has been recorded in the brain and becomes a distorting filter through which we behold each other now. So we're not together freshly and spontaneously; we're reacting to each other through the filters of our past experiences.

In childhood our parents were able to punish us by withholding what we needed for survival: affection and life-sustenance. To avoid this threat, most of us have put up with a lot from our parents. Now all of a sudden, in relationship with a partner who reminds us of one of our parents, we come upon a lot of stored up fear, anger, and vindictiveness. It may be active or passive. We may say things that we couldn't say to our elders who were all-powerful. We may rage at our companion for trying to dominate us or tell us what to do, or we may sulk with a vengeance. None of this is clear, because we're not clear about what's memory, what's image, what's the past, and what's right now.

Parents, children, you, and I—we all react in conditioned patterns most of the time. We *think* we are responding to each other consciously, spontaneously, out of the present situation, but we're not. Instead, stored-up images and programs, with their connected feelings and emotions, are constantly being triggered and projected. *They* are doing the "relating"—the reacting and the clashing.

We all have physical and psychological needs: to be touched, held, to be taken care of, to be comforted, to be loved, and so on. Do these needs dovetail in two people? Or does each person want to have his or her needs fulfilled with little regard to the needs of the other? The end result of that disregard is friction, disappointment, turning away, and maybe looking for another relationship.

Can we become aware of this whole process as it is happening, not in order to change it, but to clarify what is unclear, to bring into light what is confused and hidden?

Our usual reaction is to try to change the other person so that we can live with him or her to our own satisfaction. That is what was once done to us: "Behave, and Mom (or Dad) will love you." We were always told what to do for the sake of the peace of the parents or the family. Our parents never asked what *they* could do, at least not in our presence. They may have asked that of a therapist, but in my time parents didn't go to therapists. They knew everything! At least we thought they knew everything. They were always right, and we were always wrong.

Thus ideas and images of what we are and what others are—right or wrong, good or bad, lovable or unworthy—were programmed into our brains and bodies from the beginning. And these programs are actively functioning now in what we call our "relationship." Can we wake up to this as it is taking place? Not so that we can find fault or blame ourselves or each other; that doesn't clarify anything. Blaming only perpetuates old images.

Attention brings images to light. It clarifies without judging. With attention there can be a lightening, an opening up to each other, free of the past. Then it is no longer images that are relating to each other, but real people who have an astonishing capacity for kindness.

Attraction

We have to look at "attraction" very carefully as it happens, but that's usually the last thing we want to do at a moment of romantic excitement.

Dear Toni,

It's the morning after the retreat. Why write to you? The urge is there, and maybe something good will happen.

My companion (with whom I attended the retreat) and I have talked a lot about the hurt and ignorance in our relating to each other. But although there may still be tears and sadness, there is also a sense of investigation now. I realize that I will repeat the patterns of withdrawing and insensitivity as long as I don't understand them. My companion, too, will continue to get hurt if she depends on a relationship for happiness and completeness. So there has been a feeling of two friends talking over their problems, with the immediacy that being personally involved brings, but also with the spaciousness that comes from not being too invested in any particular outcome of the conversation, such as "We must stay together" or "Things are just not working out."

One aspect that has moved me is the question "What exactly is attraction?" A man looks at a pretty woman and wants her instead of his wife or partner. After our morning meeting with the three of us, I went out to the porch and sat in one of the big chairs. There was an unidentifiable person in the chair next to me wrapped in a blanket. After a while that person slipped down in the seat to rest his or her head against the back cushion, most likely from sheer tiredness. Perhaps feeling warm and vulnerable inside, I felt like reaching out and gently touching whoever was there. It could have been a woman, a man, maybe

---

This chapter contains Toni's response to a May 1990 letter from a retreatant. It was published in the Springwater Center Newsletter *of July 1990.*

even a dog or cat. Quickly there came the thought "What if it's the person I've been attracted to this week, the one who has brought up this old wound for my companion after a similar occurrence last year? That would be too much, especially now. Don't even dream of reaching out!" The thought wasn't quite that verbalized, but the essence was a strong prohibition, a taboo. Just as quickly after that came the almost devilish thought "Go ahead!" and for a few moments this "good and evil" battle brewed. What was clear is how desire, a thought, is strengthened by trying to prohibit or outlaw it. The thought not only escalated in the mind; it brought palpable physical tensions. Then came the realization that all this was endless and the whole matter dropped like a rock. Then there were just the birds and the rain and the breeze.

So what is attraction? It's fairly obvious that thought projects something of itself onto another person and then says it wants what the other has. Actually it wants itself. "Falling in love" is a blissful state as long as the other person doesn't dash my projections by turning out to be a real person! And the dependency on another person loving me comes after I have put onto him or her the power to take me or leave me. So subtler levels of this attraction/projection process can be seen.

All that you say about authority takes on a more direct meaning when I see the trick I am playing with thought, or rather the trick thought is playing with itself. And, as in "being in love," sorrow is inevitable. Once thought has created in me something that I want and then wanting that thought to be fulfilled, I feel divided, and I look for wholeness, completion.

So the hurt, anger, and frustration may allow further deception, keeping me from seeing what is taking place. As long as I'm angry at you, or perhaps hopeful, longing for you to be something for me, I can avoid seeing what I/thought has done to create projections and to seek fulfillment from them.

So finally this leads to the questions "What is seeing? What is aware of all this going on?" Someone said after the retreat, "I used to always be saying to myself, 'Am I doing enough?' Now after hearing Toni, I'm always wondering, 'Am I listening?'" Is this just another example of what I/thought can do, or can I truly listen or see?

There has long been a struggle with this matter of desire, since we realize that as long as that's at work, we really can't be in touch with things as they are. But then we continue to make the mistake of wanting to be without desire! Seeing things as they are includes seeing *desire*, doesn't it?

Dear ———,

Your letter raises many interesting questions.

In the beginning you write: "I will repeat the patterns of withdrawing and insensitivity as long as I don't understand them. My companion, too, will continue to get hurt if she depends on a relationship for happiness and completeness."

Is there an understanding that can really end a destructive pattern of thought, feeling, reaction?

Something can be seen very clearly at an instant—for example, the connection between a thought ("I shouldn't touch her") and an old way of reacting to that thought ("Go ahead, do it!"), with the resulting battle of "good and evil," the endlessness of that, and the letting go of it all. Unless there is direct, immediate seeing, the old patterns of insensitivity, hurt, and so on, repeat themselves every time a similar situation arises. One cannot rely on *past* understanding to prevent insensitivity and hurt *now*. The only thing that interrupts the old automatic and mechanical patterns of thought and physical reactions is the immediacy of seeing in a fresh way this very instant. That is clear.

In observing this phenomenon of "falling in love," we have to ask, "With what are we falling in love?" You say, "'Falling in love' is a blissful state as long as the other person doesn't dash my projections by turning out to be a real person!" Are thought and body actually falling in love with their own image projections? Perhaps even with remembered images?

When I find someone attractive, is it already the attracting power of an old memory image stored in the brain since the time someone with similar looks, sounds, smell, or touch aroused pleasurable feelings in this mindbody? An attractive person, particularly when he or she is looking at me in a more than casual way, may trigger the thirty thousand chemicals within, giving rise to compelling thoughts and feelings of "falling in love." But what is actually attractive and "loved" may be the sensations of excitement and energy aroused by the images of me and this other person being together.

We have to look at "attraction" very carefully as it happens, but that's usually the last thing we want to do at a moment of romantic excitement. The powerful tendency is for imagination to supply endless scenarios about me and the other person as lovers, accompanied by all the titillating as well as comforting physical sensations this organism is capable of. I "love" what the image of the other person does to me, and I "love" the resulting image of myself as loved by that person. The image taps a wellspring of pleasurable, enlivening energies that are addictive. It is also the cause of all the pain and sorrow that ensues when, as you put it, the projections turn out to be a real person; especially when instead of looking at me in an exciting way the other person ignores me and looks longingly at someone else.

Someone reading this may protest that falling in love is much more than the operation of remembered images and chemicals producing pleasurable states of body and mind. One may prefer to call it "the reenactment of the most compelling and beautiful romance of life." But is one actually interested in examining directly, meditatively, what goes on in this mind and body at the moment? We could argue indefinitely about all of our *ideas*, but is it possible to discover the truth of this moment?

You write about the dependency on a relationship for one's happiness and completeness. Why do we depend on someone to make us feel happy and complete? Is feeling happy and complete a true state, or is it an idea? We may feel happy (usually for brief periods of time) in the presence of someone who makes us feel lovable and alive, and we may become dependent on this person. But happiness turns into unhappiness or painful longing when that person is gone. This is only a description. Can it be observed directly?

Do we need to depend on anyone for feeling fully alive? Dependency and sorrow inevitably go together, that is clear. Is it possible to live alone or together lovingly, with sensitivity and aliveness, *without* dependency? We may not be able to answer this question immediately, because we need to question and look directly, patiently. So can it become a live question, shedding light on our moment-to-moment thoughts, feelings, and reactions—the incessant desires and fears, the hopes and despairs?

And what about the feeling of completeness? What is that? Is it just another energizing concept with its flickering life of belief, hope, and inspiration? Has the "I," the "me," the "self" ever felt complete without deceiving itself? It can imagine itself to be complete and derive whatever sense of fulfillment a concept is capable of arousing in this mind-body. But we are asking about more than just a concept of completion.

What is the self that yearns for completion? What is the "I" that wants something all the time—feeling insufficient and therefore wanting completeness, striving to find it, grasping to hold on to it (whatever it thinks completeness is), then fearing to lose it and suffering pain when the loss occurs? Are we really deeply interested in finding out directly? Not just thinking about it, trying to figure it all out. The insufficiency and wanting of thought will always try to complete itself through more thought and imagination.

You wrote in your letter that at some instant the realization came "that all this was endless and the whole matter dropped like a rock. Then there were just the birds and the rain and the breeze." At that moment of complete listening, without wanting, where is the idea of completion?

"What is seeing? What is aware of all this going on?" you may ask. Seeing is without any sense of "I" or "me," without any sense of thought of completeness or incompleteness. It is without a shadow of division. It is birds calling, rain dropping, the breeze rustling, trees swaying, the heart beating, the back aching, thoughts arising and disappearing, people walking, sitting—all of that and none of that. Not the words, not the concepts, not any separation. There is no one there to be aware, so there is no *thought* of awareness, yet everything there is as it is, whole, without desire. When the thought "I want this" comes up, can it simply be seen? Desire can be seen, and in that seeing there is no desire. When questions arise—"Am I truly seeing?" "Am I truly listening?"—what is happening? Is this thought about thought? Or is it just a moment of simple listening, openly, without knowing?

Fact and Story Line

Why are we constantly pursuing a dream? Why are we pursuing what is unreal rather than being directly in touch with what is actually happening?

Dear Toni,

I am a woman in a houseful of men, seeking peace. That is roughly equivalent to living in Nazi Germany and seeking peace. What is peace? My problem is to discover the balance between activism and acceptance, confrontation and love. Anyway, that's how it seems to me.

There are five men in this house, and me. Sometimes I manage to get one or two of them to fairly full participation for days at a time, but never all of them. I have tried so many things to get the kids (all adults now) to accept responsibility, but our society quietly teaches them that the meals and clothes and dust and worries are my job—me, the woman and mother. I cannot let that go on. It is unjust, so fundamentally unjust that perhaps everything else unjust in the world starts with that one dropped towel. I know there must be a way—there just must be, if flowers grow and the wind blows—to find the balance. And if I can, so too can countries solve injustice.

So much more is involved than just smiling while requesting that the towel be picked up. I am hoping that you understand how I feel, how my sons react to me when I make demands on them, and how this affects me.

This seems shameful and silly, writing it down on paper. Imagine putting it on a par with racism. I am tempted sometimes to just give up,

This chapter contains Toni's response to an undated letter. It was published in the Springwater Center Newsletter *of April 1991.*

put on the apron, meditate, smile, love them (as I do), cook my head off, and accept it as my job in life (along with my full-time teaching job, writing, aerobics, and my husband). If I could just accept it, there would be a lot less heartache. I wouldn't have the shame I feel from having to continually "make a scene"—because that is how they see any confrontation on my part, no matter how gently I approach them, and I see it the same way.

So that, in a nutshell, is my life, I have been reading as much as I can about Zen, and I get up early to meditate for a half hour.

Do you think there is some way I could get guidance from you? I really need help, and I hope I have a sincere desire to overcome self and be of genuine service to the world.

Dear ———,

Rather than trying to seek solutions, overcome the self, or be of genuine service to the world, can we as human beings, caught in the midst of endless confrontation and fighting or weary acceptance of things, begin with a completely different approach: listening quietly and feeling inwardly all that's going on in and around us, without either acceptance or rejection?

Our present human condition appears intolerable to most of us most of the time. Globally we are caught in massive deception, war, destruction, and killing, and in the home there is little or no peace and love either, as your letter clearly describes. So what are we going to do? Where are we going to begin?

I am no giver of advice, comfort, or inspirational cheer. Rather I am asking with you what is one to do in the midst of all this ongoing chaos? How is one to deal with the ever accumulating conflict and sorrow, anger, resentment, fear, and self-pity, for all these pit us one against another?

Can we question this together right now, as friends, or are we each pursuing our own thoughts and aims? If we pursue this separately, we cannot explore together openly, innocently, from the very outset.

So can we start fresh, not knowing where the inquiry will take us, and not demanding from the beginning a desirable outcome? All we know is that we feel great conflict, distress, and pain in ourselves and in relationship with the people around us, and we don't want to continue living that way. But we really don't know what another way of living would be like.

You ask, "What is peace?" Does peace actually exist anywhere, or is it just an imagined, glorified state that we think about and desire desperately for ourselves and others? We talk and write about peace, we long for it, work, march, fight, and sacrifice for it, but it eludes us forever, like an unattainable dream. Why?

Why are we constantly pursuing a dream? Why are we pursuing what is unreal rather than being directly in touch with what is actually happening? You describe it in your letter: the lack of participation and involvement by members of your family in keeping order, your being overworked, the "scenes," the lack of understanding, the frustration, and the ongoing *story lines* emerging in your brain about your painful life replete with injustice.

Does the retelling, the portraying of our living situation to ourselves and others, trigger torrents of feelings? Feelings of hurt, resentment, depression, despair? Do thoughts and images constantly poured out by the brain *about* our "fate" act like loaded, provocative headlines that arouse intense emotions for and against each other?

What I'm trying to say is this: first there are the facts of our present living situation—in your case, living in a houseful of men, enduring their lack of neatness, their lack of participation in housework, and the social pressures you feel as a woman to assume the role of cleaner, cook, caregiver, and so on. Second, there is also the way we *perceive* all of this, think and feel about it, and describe it to ourselves in words that arouse intense emotions. Is it possible to see the difference between what is actually happening and the way we are *describing* it to ourselves? Strong emotions are aroused not only by factual circumstances, but also by the way in which the ongoing story lines and images in the brain *portray* these circumstances, comment on them, and stir up increasing reaction and agitation.

Let me give you an example. Recently I came into the kitchen where my husband Kyle had already prepared some food for himself (he was on a special diet at the time). I had expected to find something fixed for me too, but he hadn't fixed anything for me. These were the facts. Not simply letting it go at that, thoughts with strong overtones emerged instead: "No one ever does anything for me!" A catchy headline, but not the truth. With the internal comment that no one ever does anything for me came a welling up of emotion that was about to affect the whole organism. But somehow I saw this unfolding process directly, just before it erupted into spoken words. The agitation collapsed, and the relationship with Kyle remained friendly, undisturbed by self-pity and accusation. What is seen clearly needn't be suppressed; it takes care of itself.

Please do not misunderstand me as saying, "Put up with your situation. Don't think about it. It's all your problem. It's only in your head. There is no justice or injustice. Just sit and meditate," and so on. This is *not* what I'm saying.

Right now can we just examine together what is actually going on when a towel has been dropped carelessly? The towel was dropped by your son; that is a fact. There it is, lying on the floor where you feel it does not belong. What else is happening almost simultaneously? Are there quick remembrances of countless other times when towels and other things were dropped carelessly? Times when you have asked that someone please not drop things on the floor, times when you have not been heard, have been opposed or disregarded, . . . when you have not gotten your way, . . . have given in, . . . times, perhaps, when your mother reprimanded you for the same thing, and the ways in which she and you reacted to each other then, . . . uncountable times of feeling humiliated, dominated, victimized, and then sorry for yourself? The present instance triggers the whole past.

And what is going on for your son? Usually we only think through our side of the story but know little or nothing of the other side. Our own story is so overpowering that there is little space and energy left for listening to others, putting ourselves in their shoes. What happens when we begin to wonder how others feel, and how they have come to do or say what is so upsetting to us now? Can we listen quietly, carefully?

Most of the time the habitual grooves on all sides prevail, and hurt, confrontation, feelings of shame and indifference continue. But every once in a while there may be an astonishing glimpse into how the perception of a fact—the towel on the floor—or, rather, the story line about the fact, is about to turn into an explosive problem. This glimpse may actually diffuse the problem before it has affected the entire organism and everyone else as well. This glimpse or insight throws light on the birth and death of a problem; but it also calls into question the whole problem of "self." Is this suffering "I" the result of past and present thought-feelings that powerfully affect the entire organism?

All of us—men, women, grown-ups, and children alike—are caught up in deeply conditioned grooves of behaving and reacting that make sustained peaceful living all but impossible. Can we see and acknowledge this fact? Can we take some quiet time with it, patiently, whenever it crops up? When we discover not just other people's pain-producing habits but also our own lack of freedom to respond spontaneously, lovingly, a new kind of intelligence and kindliness may begin to unfold in our relationships.

Examining what is going on in this way, the important question may no longer be "Who is to blame?" or "What did I or someone else do wrong?" but rather "What is it that keeps us immersed in feelings of separation, noncaring, violence, and sorrow?" Can this question be pondered deeply?

The light of insight is the seed of kindliness and peace.

Prejudice

*Do I feel separation between "myself" and "the others"? It may
be very subtle, but there it is. Judging others as good or evil,
right or wrong, valuable or worthless creates division between
"myself" as judge, and "others" as judged.*

Dear Toni,

Sometimes it feels as though acute perception is an aspect of the "critical mind." It is judgmental and harsh, with myself, with others, with
the whole human race. What is awareness, what is criticism (judgment), and what is merely discernment? And does one offer the presence of awareness—to others? in speaking? in writing?

For instance, at Quaker meeting last Sunday, two people spoke of
their pride and joy at being Quakers these days, in heartfelt speeches.
(Quaker meeting consists of a shared silence for meditation or prayer.
People are free to stand and share thoughts and insights, and then the
speaker sits down, and the group is again silent together.) In the end,
I had to stand and offer the perception, quoting James Baldwin: "You
have to stop being white; as long as you're white, I'm black." And
I said, because I felt it acutely, listening to myself, "Hear how the
'I'-word makes such a claim. I am this. I am not this. Such fierceness."
I feel the same fierceness in writing and speaking. I want myself and
all of us to change. It is a violent wish. Or is it? Something must die in
order for us to be freed. How does one point these insights out to others? Or do we simply share silence, letting awareness come and go as
it will?

*This chapter contains Toni's response to a February 1991 letter from a friend. It
was published in the* Springwater Center Newsletter *of July 1991.*

Dear ———,

Can a human being share silence with others and also speak and write out of silence without becoming somebody in the process—a proud Quaker, Buddhist, or "Meditative Inquirer"? Can one do so without creating any opposition between "me" and "them," and without fiercely wishing that oneself and all others would change? You sense violence in this wish to change, but you also question it. To probe into this, we have to go deep.

Do I feel separation between "myself" and "the others"? It may be very subtle, but there it is. Judging others as good or evil, right or wrong, valuable or worthless creates division between "myself" as judge, and "others" as judged. Violence emerges out of this division. Division is violence. Can this be seen clearly as it happens?

When I feel superior to others, the need arises to convince them of my superiority, to want them to acknowledge my better ideas and ways, or to make them conform. All this can be carefully observed in our daily living together, at home, in a place of worship, at work, with friends, and also between ethnic, racial, tribal, national, or any other groups.

Can there be awareness (discernment) of the many differences in our physical appearances, backgrounds, capacities, education, beliefs, traditions, moral standards, and so on, without any (pre)judgment? Not "Yes, there can be," or "No, there can't be." Rather can we carefully feel out and question this constant sense of separation in ourselves that gives rise to our constant judging of others? Can we feel directly how judging strengthens the sense of a separate "I"? At the very moment that it comes up, can we see the sense of separation without judging it, without the "I" taking a position for or against what is simply seen to be so?

You asked, "What is awareness, what is criticism (judgment), and what is merely discernment?" And can something be shared without bringing about new conflict, without fierceness, without violence?

Let's make a fresh start using your example of "white" and "black." White skin is distinguishable from dark skin, but if no value whatsoever were attached to white or black, consciously or unconsciously, would the mere discernment of such differences create a feeling of separation, a judgment of superiority or inferiority? How can we even test this out when many of us are so deeply conditioned to regard "white" and "light" as intrinsically superior to "black" and "dark"? Conscious as well as unconscious prejudice against human beings of different looks and behaviors has been deeply programmed in us from very early times. Can we get glimpses into this conditioning in ourselves? Can we stop clinging to the idea of each of us being a person without any prejudice and instead really become aware of the many subtle reactions we register in contacts with people who look and act differently from us?

Can we share deeply in wondering whether prejudice with all its divisiveness and sorrow can end in each of us? Questioning freely whether judging can end in oneself has nothing to do with condemning judgment, nor with condoning or suppressing it. Questioning can occur when we are seeing directly and feeling acutely the suffering springing from constantly judging ourselves and others. It is wondering about it all in a deep way: Why is this happening all the time? Does it inevitably have to continue this way? Is there a root cause of all this, and can one come upon it directly? We are not demanding an instant answer to these questions, but we can allow them to illumine the moment-to-moment judging without making any further judgment.

Can we see, speak, and write out of the silence of wondering without knowing? Can words flow out of the stillness of listening and looking, without thought immediately creating the perceiving, judging, valuing, self-important or worthless "I" and "you"?

You write, "Something must die in order for us to be freed." What is this something that must die?

The differences that appear in "you" and "me," in our looks, behavior, background, talents, or whatever, are undeniably there and can be seen for what they are. Seeing freely what is there is not the same as judging or condoning. What is there, and its consequences, speaks for itself when there is quiet listening, so let it speak for itself. Can quiet, open listening/seeing be the dying to self-centered opposition—dying to the separation between "you" and "me"? Can we behold the differences in human beings with the same wonder and love as beholding the million colors, shapes, sounds, and fragrances of a fresh spring day?

Awareness and Fear

At the first sign of scary, disagreeable physical thoughts and feelings, why not stop *and* attend? *It's not impossible! Fear and discomfort can be powerful waker-uppers: "What is going on right now?"*

Every one of us is familiar with fear. Or we *think* we are familiar with it. Maybe we are not. We have just experienced uncomfortable, scary physical sensations, which accompany fearful thoughts about the future or frightful past memories: "I've failed at everything. I've never finished anything. I probably will fail again." And there are the physical manifestations that are mobilized by such thoughts in the solar plexus, the intestines, the stomach. The heart beats faster. The senses narrow down. One doesn't see or hear what one saw and heard a moment before. There's no relaxation. The muscles are tensing up.

Are we intimate with this whole physical movement of fear? Or do we just label it "fear," say, "I don't want to feel this way," and then try everything possible to get away from it, not to experience it? When fear and anxiety actually come into awareness, there is a precious opportunity to experience the whole thing, to go through it completely from beginning to end without any need for escape.

We may think there was no thought or memory that caused the fear: "I can't remember any thought. I'm just anxious all the time." But what *maintains* it? What *sustains* this feeling of anxiety? Aren't memories involved in some way? Thoughts? The story line about me and my life is running. I am evaluating myself, judging, "I did wrong. I'm no good. I'm hopeless." I'm experiencing fearful notions of what will happen in the future. "Will I have a job? Will I have old-age insurance when I get sick? Will somebody take care of me when I die?"

This chapter was adapted from a retreat talk of February 1994 and was published in the Springwater Center Newsletter *of July 1994.*

Imagining scenarios with their running comments keeps our bodies producing what we have learned to call "fear"—disagreeable symptoms, which the body does not want to feel. Thought doesn't like fear either. It says, "Go away. I can't stand it." Resistance causes more physical symptoms, symptoms of conflict. A fearful memory triggers physical mobilization to run, fight, or freeze, and then conflict ensues. The mindbody is bracing against itself: "I don't like this. I don't want to feel this way." Tension increases. And then there is anxiety about this spiralling condition. More frightening thoughts come up: "This is getting worse. How is it going to end?" And there are renewed physical symptoms in response to all these troubling thoughts.

At the first sign of scary, disagreeable physical thoughts and feelings, why not *stop* and *attend*? It's not impossible! Fear and discomfort can be powerful waker-uppers: "What is going on right now?"

I can't do it for anyone else. But awareness happens for everyone when there is the interest and readiness to be in touch directly, immediately, without description or explanation or diagnosis. When there is intimate touch with what is happening right here, this moment, without any separation. No escape. Going for broke, come what may. Touching, feeling that fear, the anger, the jealousy—whatever we may have learned to call it.

It's an astonishing and lightening moment when separation ends. Separation *is* this thinking: "I can't bear it. It's too much for me. Too dangerous." Once this physical-mental resistance is directly discovered, it does not continue. Awareness takes its place. It's like an exchange of energy.

Then what *is* pain, fear, anger, anxiety as it is manifesting *right now*, without naming it, without knowing it? What is it directly, immediately?

The significant thing is not *what* it is that is touched and discovered, but that there is *no separation* in being. Then *whatever* is touched changes. Whatever is there is not the same anymore when it is unconditionally allowed to be there in the fullness of awareness, when one is no longer looking for loopholes or escape routes.

No separation. There is only what's manifesting here right now, and now, and now and now—a free flow of events without anyone doing or controlling or escaping. Not knowing. But being there with it all. It's a simple shift from thinking about ourselves and the world to *just being here*.

What is it that we're afraid of? Sometimes in talking about pure awareness being truly undefinable, wholly unnameable, open without any boundaries, no inside or outside, people say, "This sounds scary to me. I feel fear right now as you speak about this." Trying to imagine *not* existing the way we habitually *think* we do triggers fear. It's a strange paradox that there's fear of existing as well as fear of not existing. Fear of dying as well as fear of living. And by "living" I mean "being here," directly, immediately, not as this or that person, not as bundles of memory about what I am or what I'm going to be, but *pure, simple being*.

Why does being here arouse fear? Is it the same as the fear of dying? Why this fear of pure awareness, pure hereness, nowness? Is pure awareness actually the *same* as dying? So therefore we have the same fear about it?

Fear of loss of what I know—my personality, my incarnation, my personal past, my possessions, my pleasures and attachments, my future—is all of that called into question, already sensed and mourned as a loss, when we talk about being *here*, fully aware? Can one realize right now that fear at the thought of pure awareness and fear at the thought of dying are all caused by fantasy and speculation? One doesn't know what it means to die. And one may not really know firsthand what it is to be fully here now.

Why is there this strong identification with *this* person I call "me," this mind with its remembered history, it's self-images, and this body I call "my own"? Why this tremendously strong identification and attachment to it all? Is that worth questioning? Is identification with and attachment to this mindbody the very root source of fear? Without attachment to ourselves, what would there be to worry and tremble about?

Why are we so identified with our life story? Why not just let there be simple awareness of what's happening—happy moments, fearful thoughts, angry feelings, sad memories, work well done, mistakes made—without weaving it all into more story? Thought is always stepping into the picture as "me," the main character—damming up the stream of events with self-reference, reacting and commenting and emoting about "myself"—becoming attached to what is experienced and felt as "good me," and rejecting of what is judged as "bad me": "I don't want to be that way. This is not me. I don't like it." We are clinging, denying, or escaping from ourselves all the time.

Where are we right now? What are we? Is it possible to observe these ever-changing states of feelings and emotions dispassionately *without becoming the owner or dis-owner of any of them?*

Pure awareness is the essence of what we truly are. We are not the different states and feelings, moods and tempers succeeding one another. All of it comes and goes lightly, cloudlike, without leaving a trace, when thought doesn't identify with any of it.

To be here now is just to see, just to hear, to experience it all like the plane humming [an airplane is flying overhead] without needing to become anything. All listening, without being a listener.

Why does this seem to be so hard? We're *so* deeply programmed to imagine ourselves as being the experiencer, or victim, of all these passing states of mindbody. We don't know anything else, or at least we think we don't. But awareness is here. Simply being here is clear, isn't it? We're present right now, aren't we? Where else could we be but right here! Isn't that clear?

One is not being *this* or *that*—that's something extra, added on by thought. One is not becoming entangled in the extras. There is just experiencing the pureness of being. Awake. Heart beating, voice sounding, leg aching, breathing in, out, in, out, body moving gently with the breathing. Helicopter buzzing. It's all *here*. Directly, immediately here. One is not separate from awareness. Nothing is separate. Awareness is all.

In the immediacy of being awake and present, totally unnameable and undefinable, empty of all self-reference, there is no fear about not continuing, because there is nothing there to continue. There is only what's here now, all of it now. And that's always new and fresh from moment to moment.

When thinking starts up, "How will I be tomorrow, happy or unhappy?" the story spins out again, and with it the fear of not making it or losing it, or not lasting forever. Or the fear that pure awareness means I'm going to be dead, like a stone. Stones aren't dead either.

So what is there, right now, when there's *no* identification with anything? It's just what it is!

What am I, this very moment, without knowing?

Being Here Now: An Interview

Life energy can be right here in all-embracing awakeness,
without the hindrances of all our thought-created divisions.
It's possible for anyone to come into this state of being, which is
true being.

JACEK: Toni, you work with people in America, Germany, Britain,
Sweden, Holland, and in Poland, where you've been coming since
1975. You stress that in spite of individual and national differences,
we're all very much alike as human beings, and that the differences are
only on the surface. But they still seem very big. As far as the images of
national identity go, as far as temperament goes, Poland is a Catholic,
mother-oriented culture, and other countries you visit are more Protes-
tant, father-oriented in nature. Is it easier for you to work with Germans since you're of German background? Are Germans really more
serious and diligent? Are Americans really more practical and less ideological than Europeans? Are the Swiss more introverted? Are Poles
more messy? Or are these just clichés, and the similarities are greater
than the differences?

TONI: I had to laugh when you listed all these different characteris-
tics that sound like clichés. They can probably be found among any of
the people who come to retreats. It's true that there are varying cultural
backgrounds and personality differences; they are just part and parcel
of our *general* conditioning, which is what's really important to become
deeply aware of. No, I don't feel that it's easier for me to work with
Germans. Most of the people I meet and work with in retreats in
America and abroad are, in a way, more familiar to me than the people

This interview by Jacek Dobrowoloski took place in Warsaw, in November
1993. Jacek, a poet and translator, acts as Toni's interpreter during her workshops
and retreats in Poland.

I grew up with. I actually had no experience with meditation or spiritual life during my youth and adolescence. When I came back to Germany to give talks and meetings, it was like having to learn a new language.

So coming back to your initial question, when we are sitting quietly, listening spaciously, observing what is happening from moment to moment, differences from one country to another disappear.

JACEK: What about differences in emotional expression?

TONI: Differences in emotional expression...

JACEK: From one nation to another.

TONI: I really couldn't say anything about that, not in this kind of work where you spend lots of quiet time and look rather deeply within. Anger may come up. Fear may arise. Or boredom. Longing and wanting are stirring most all the time. There is no German anger, or Polish fear, Swedish boredom, Dutch wanting, or English longing. Fear is fear, anger is anger, even if the objects of fear and anger vary from one person or country to the next. The openness of quiet listening is not culturally conditioned, though the blockages are.

JACEK: I see that. To take up another point, Springwater Center seems very democratic. You avoid dominating it. Anyone can give talks during retreats when you are not there, or when you are just a retreat participant [in January each year]. There's no set hierarchy. Do you feel that the work done in such a place, in such a community, is an antidote to the spiritual and political tyrannies all over the world?

TONI: I don't think in terms of opposites or antidotes. We're just doing—I'm just doing—what I cannot help doing. In working together, it seems natural to listen to each other carefully, openly, trying to understand what someone else is trying to say, without already knowing answers. I deeply feel the importance of letting everyone express their ideas and feelings when we have to make a decision. It's much better that we've all heard each other, heard lots of suggestions, lots of facts, maybe lots of emotions, rather than having a few people decide things in isolation.

JACEK: Yes, I remember attending one of the meetings of the staff. The atmosphere was really excellent. I've been to many such meetings at various centers, and the one at Springwater was certainly the most amiable and caring and respectful. So this is very beautiful.

TONI: It's amazing how people who work together over a period of time can really learn to listen to each other, although it is not easy. We're not used to listening to each other. We are under great pressure from our own ideas with which we are deeply, mostly unconsciously, identified. We want to promote our ideas and ourselves at the same time. There is no listening space when we're just waiting to get our point of view across. Listening quietly to what someone else has to say, without interrupting, is something rare, and yet it can happen. The capacity to listen can develop over a period of time, with patience. There is a lot of strength in it.

JACEK: So besides being a center of meditative inquiry, Springwater can also be seen as a school of democracy.

TONI: That sounds much too conceptual, too ideological. Whatever happens is rather a natural unfolding of being and working caringly alone and together.

JACEK: Why do we frequently object to external political or religious tyrannies and so easily succumb to spiritual ones?

TONI: Yes, I've wondered about this myself. Many people come to spiritual traditions out of revolt against the tyranny and suffering they have experienced in a repressive political or religious system. Why then submit to spiritual authority? Do we actually realize it when it is happening, or does it remain unconscious? Do we believe, or are we made to believe by teachers, that authority in spiritual matters is different from other kinds of authority, and that it is indispensable for a spiritual seeker? Do we believe that there is something sacrosanct about spiritual teachers, a kind of untouchableness? Infallibility? Omniscience? Perfection? In many churches, temples, and spiritual centers the place occupied by the priest or teacher is carefully kept apart from the space where ordinary people congregate.

We love to identify with personages to whom we have attributed special powers. It makes us feel a bit more empowered ourselves. Some people really get angry with me when I say that I do not intend to be an authority for them, that what I communicate is for everyone to question, examine, and discover through direct insight. No one can discover truth for another. Some people respond angrily to this, saying, "But I *do need* authority. I *want* you to be my teacher. You're disappointing me."

JACEK: They want security.

TONI: We want security, yes, and power through identification. Maybe for some of us it's a re-creation of childhood, when we could hold our parents' hands and unthinkingly trust in their protection and omniscience.

JACEK: A different question. Here in Poland, doctors very rarely tell terminally ill patients that they're going to die. They justify this practice by saying that most people wouldn't be able to cope with the knowledge. Isn't that an excuse for lying, and doesn't it show that the doctors really aren't able to cope with the situation themselves?

TONI: My husband and I have thought about this question of terminal illness and whether one should know about it, because he has had cancer, which is now in remission. From our own scant research it seems that very often doctors don't really know for sure whether an illness is terminal or not—there are cases of astounding remission. So what can one really say? One doctor wrote that some patients die from their diagnosis. If I were a doctor I wouldn't lie to someone out of fear that he or she couldn't cope with the truth, but I would wonder, Do I really know the truth? I wouldn't be so sure of the accuracy of prognoses based on past experience. What is certain is that we cannot know what will happen to any of us the next moment, the next day, or the next year.

Now the assumption that the patient can't cope with the thought of dying needs to be questioned, doesn't it? The doctor himself may not be able to cope with the idea of death. Many doctors are unquestioningly committed to prolonging life and fighting death at all costs. Death is regarded as something horrible to be postponed as long as possible, no matter what suffering this may entail for the patient. So if the doctor is afraid of death, how can he or she be at ease with a dying person?

JACEK: Exactly. Also there's a question of the doctor as an authority figure. The doctor, as all professionals, cannot say he doesn't know, so he may not say anything.

TONI: Yes. Very often patients are wiser than their doctors. They may—

JACEK: Have premonitions. . . .

TONI: Yes.

JACEK: But then both sides frequently play the game of pretending.

TONI: Recently two very close friends of mine died, both of cancer. Neither of them accepted any treatments like radiation or chemotherapy. One didn't take any painkillers at all. Both wanted to die fully aware. Both were cared for by their loved ones at home and passed away without heroic measures, without even a doctor attending. Neither pain nor fear seemed to become problems. The assumption that death is something horrible to be afraid of needs to be thoroughly questioned.

JACEK: Yes. What advice, Toni, would you give to a dying person?

TONI: Right at this moment I don't know what I would say. I would have to be right there. Neither of my friends were really asking me for advice. They were rather appreciating my unconditional presence, by letter or by phone.

JACEK: Yes.

TONI: Being present, being here. Without fear. Without ideas. Not wanting anything for oneself. I frequently talked with one of the friends over the phone, and in the beginning we were laughing a lot, and she said she was not afraid of dying. She had known for a long time that she would not live. She had asked her husband if in her hours of dying he would call me up and hold the phone to her ear so I could talk to her. He did it faithfully. One time when he called up, I just heard her breathing, no more words, just breathing. And then one day he called and said, "She just stopped breathing," but I still talked to her.

JACEK: Yes.

TONI: And . . . I don't recall now what I said, but it was something like, "There's nothing to be afraid of. There's nothing to hold onto. No place to go. Everything is right here. We're all home."

JACEK: Yes. So you feel people who are dying, who have started the work of inquiry, of questioning, should pursue it, should be extra attentive?

TONI: Be attentive *now*, yes. And to realize clearly, while we're still healthy and with energy, that we're not just this mindbody. Our strong identification with the mindbody as a separate entity, divided within and apart from other people, separate from nature, from the universe, this identification and separation is simply false. Each one of us can come upon truth directly. So while we are living, can there be dying to the false assumptions of what I am, leaving it completely open? Can there be just wondering, deeply, silently, without knowing, really questioning what I am? Ideas and assumptions can suddenly give way to something wholly quiet, empty, timeless, and pure—the essence permeating everything.

JACEK: And that is deathless and indestructible.

TONI: That's right. That's right. Deathless and birthless. It is realizable in this life *before* we die physically. You may recall, I don't know who said these beautiful words—

JACEK: "Those who die before they die do not die when they die"?

TONI: Yes, that's right. Yes.

JACEK: Do you have any foreknowledge of how long you're going to live? I'm not asking you to tell us. But if not, are you at all interested in finding out?

TONI: No. I'm not interested in finding out. And I don't have foreknowledge. Right now I feel very healthy and alive and energetic, and this mind doesn't occupy itself with such thoughts.

JACEK: Are you interested?

TONI: Do you mean, if I knew of someone who could predict the date of my death, would I seek him or her out and ask?

JACEK: Because if you knew you could organize your life more meticulously, and perhaps it's such valuable information, perhaps everyone should really be interested in trying to ask or inquire about it.

TONI: I understand your question better now. But I feel the joy of meticulous order *now* from moment to moment.

JACEK: Yes, you're very well organized and spontaneous at the same time, and very joyful. I've known you for many years, and for me, it is proof of, well, your inner strength that seeing so much pain and pointing it out nevertheless does not disturb your aliveness and the joy of every moment.

TONI: It need not. When the thought comes about dying, or somebody like you asks about death, I say, well, of course, there'll be a time of dying, and that's what will be happening right then without anything needing to be different. In asking advice about our moment to moment living and dying, . . . if we can be wholly what is, without wanting it otherwise, then all is well. All *is* well!

JACEK: Yes, yes. Can I ask something else? You had said, I remember, quite recently that you've never met a person without ego. Do you mean to say that such people do not exist or that they're extremely rare or not found among spiritual teachers in the present age?

TONI: It is entirely possible for human beings like you and me to be here without constantly thinking about ourselves, worrying about ourselves, projecting ourselves, needing to be or become someone important or unimportant. The life energy need not necessarily be caught up in this vast, millennia-old network of "me-ness" with its imagery, identifications, memories, desires, fears, and illusory security. Life energy can be right here in all-embracing awakeness, without the hindrances of all our thought-created divisions. It's possible for anyone to come into this state of being, which is true being. What I meant was that I don't know of anyone who is in that state *all the time.*

JACEK: Right. Right.

TONI: But this is what we always want—

JACEK: We have an idea—

TONI: Have an idea and project perfection onto someone, because for some reason there seems to be such a great need in us to know of people who are perfect, to worship them, become identified with them, or to be afraid of them. One is afraid of not measuring up to their attainment, and therefore one is hard on oneself, judgmental of imperfections, because there are these people who are so perfect, and one thinks, "Why can't I be like them?" That's why it is so helpful to let go of the ideal of the perfected human being, so that this mad circuit of constant comparison and self-judgment abates. Then one can instead be in touch with what one really is and what everyone else really is at this instant. Does that make sense?

JACEK: Yes, the habit of constant comparing should be abandoned.

TONI: It should be seen through. Can there be transparency about what is going on right now? About comparisons—creating ideals, comparing ourselves to these ideals, then either feeling superior or inferior and suffering from the emotional effects of judgment throughout the entire organism?

JACEK: Thank you. That's it.

TONI: That's the whole thing?

JACEK: Yes.

TONI: Good.

Observing What Is

Thoughts evoke emotions, tensions, excitement, and stress, and can bring on exhaustion and sickness. Awareness reveals this simply to be so.

Dear Toni,

Last summer I took part in a seven-day retreat at Springwater. It seemed clear to me then that there is no thinker, only thought.

At this time I'm teaching second grade and am taking "myself" too seriously. Perhaps just phrasing things like that reflects that the awareness of no-thinker is only skin-deep.

Worries about how the kids are doing, especially because I have some who are very needy, and worries about how I am doing are still there. And I want to impress people, want to stand out.

Many times I can be aware of this stuff as thoughts, but nonetheless these concerns affect my sleep. I don't sleep well. Then I get physically and emotionally run-down and sick. It's as though something hasn't sunk in. Maybe I'm just expecting things to be better because I think I am aware.

Sometimes I think about leaving teaching because it demands so much, or perhaps I have an unhealthy relationship to it: I seem to be looking for satisfaction of the desire for recognition, praise, and affection. At the same time, it seems like the ideal place for insight to occur—but then it doesn't. I just get sick.

Teaching is like a black hole that sucks all one has to give, leaving nothing. But perhaps it's not really the teaching but the "self" that is the black hole, that is insatiable. Perhaps that is what is meant by the words "hungry ghost."

This chapter contains Toni's response to a November 1991 letter from a retreatant. It was published in the Springwater Center Newsletter *of October 1992.*

Dear ———,

Much of what you state in your letter comes out of direct observation: Taking "myself" too seriously, worrying about how I am doing, wanting to impress people, realizing that these thoughts and their connected emotions disturb sleep, that lack of sleep results in physical and emotional drain, expecting things to be better because one thinks one is aware, and then again feeling disappointed that "awareness" doesn't seem to help. Something feels like a "black hole," but is it teaching or the "self" that is insatiable?

What does one do with all these direct observations? Our habitual response is to wish things were different from the way they are. We wish things were better, progressively improving, or as good as they were at times of clarity in the past. But moment-to-moment awareness only throws clear light on what is—it has no reactions, comparisons, prescriptions, or remedies for improvement. Wisdom about how we live, alone, and with each other, comes out of direct observation, not out of thinking how things should or should not be. And when awareness prevails at times without giving way to judgment for or against, it clarifies that just being in the closest of touch with inner and outer conditions as they are has its own wisdom. Everyone can come upon this wisdom.

All of us, without exception, have been thoroughly conditioned to react immediately to what is happening in and around us by thinking about it—talking to ourselves and to others in judgmental ways, often repeating these thoughts over and over again. Thoughts evoke emotions, tensions, excitement, and stress, and can bring on exhaustion and sickness. Awareness reveals this simply to be so.

Is it totally radical to just stop, look, listen, and experience what is actually taking place without immediately reacting with more thinking about it all? Can there be just a simple awareness, which means experiencing openly, innocently, this whole stream without getting caught up in thoughts about what is good, what could be better or perhaps worse?

Awareness is not progressive; it illumines *what is* without a sense of time, without self-separation. By "self-separation" I mean the mechanism of evaluating how I am doing, whether I am impressing others or am disapproved of by an imagined audience (which includes myself), and the inner tensions that go with all of this. Separation is thinking about better or worse states in the future or past. Awareness is freedom from wanting to improve oneself or to put oneself down. It illumines habitual thinking-feeling patterns and simultaneously opens one up to whatever else is happening this instant: breathing, a bird singing, a motor humming, the wind blowing, thoughts moving, the body tensing and relaxing. . . .

What are we without thinking about ourselves all the time? What are we when we are simply looking, listening, experiencing choicelessly what is there in this infinite space of aliveness?

Thought

As we all find out, going over and over our problems and trying to seek mental solutions doesn't work. It just becomes a repetitive, circular, looping thing. And, of course, every time we think of our problems, the whole body is upset, one way or another. Can one see for oneself that with psychological problems, thinking, trying to come up with a solution, does not bring the ending of the problem? One needs to find out for oneself the limitations of thinking—where it is appropriate, where it can do something, and where it becomes circular, looping around and around and around.

Can thought alone understand this, or to see it does one already need insight—insight into thought and its limitations? I don't know. Some say thought can see its limitations. My perception is that thought can only *think* about its limitations—it can't SEE! Thought doesn't see—it's *thinking*! But thought looping round and round can be seen: insight reveals it clearly, and the futility of it. The solution of the problem lies in *seeing* it—in the seeing, without wanting a solution, or dissolution—just seeing what's there. . . .

This seeing is not watching in the way that we usually think about it—with "me" always there as the watcher. Seeing has no seer involved in it, no watcher, no observer. It's open like the sky, just revealing what's there without any sense of separation or judgment.

This chapter was adapted from a talk delivered in June 1991.

The Quest for Enlightenment

Would there be any quest for enlightenment if it weren't for our sense of time? Time is created by thought, memory, and imagination: what I was, what I am, what I will be. Forever feeling insufficient and lacking, we want to become whole and complete in the future. We will submit to any spiritual path to overcome our hindrances in the course of time. Then, we imagine hopefully, there will come the day when we will experience enlightenment, the liberation from bondage that has been promised to us by the traditions of the past.

I don't think in terms of having experiences any more. Things just happen. Rain is dripping softly. The heart is beating. There is breathing, in-out-in-out-in-out. There is quiet listening, openness . . . emptiness . . . nothing. . . .

Enlightenment? How lethal it is to attach a label. Then you become somebody. At the moment of labelling, aliveness freezes into a concept. "My enlightenment experience!" To be alive, fully alive, means flowing without hindrance—a vulnerable flow of aliveness with no resistance. Without any sense of passing time. Without needing to think about "myself"—what I am, what I will be. Our experience mongering is a form of resistance in time.

Our craving for experiences is a resistance to simply being here, now. It's the hum of the airplane. The fog. The wind blowing gently, the rain dripping, breathing, humming, pulsating, opening, closing, nothing at all. . . .

It's such a relief to realize we don't have to be anything.

This chapter was adapted from a talk delivered in June 1991 and was published in the Springwater Center Newsletter *of October 1992.*

Psychotherapy and Spiritual Practice

Disturbing emotional or behavioral symptoms do not necessarily prevent one from doing meditative work. And meditative work need not necessarily become an escape into stillness and a retreat from the pain and turmoil of psychological problems.

QUESTIONER: As a psychotherapist working with people with moderately severe problems, I don't think that working on the illusion of the existence of a "separate me" would constitute what Buddhism calls "skillful means,"* even though that path might help resolve suffering. I myself have been working in Zen practice with the koan Mu for ten years without a "solution."

The people I work with are simply too distressed (as I myself have been) to put aside their worldly suffering in the hopes of seeing into the illusory nature of a "separate me" as *the* means of dealing with their frequently very intense suffering. The suffering is often so intense that putting it aside to pursue the central spiritual question is not possible.

For me psychotherapy has been necessary and helpful over and above (or beside) my spiritual practice. I'm trying to see what methods and insights from spiritual practice can be useful in a psychotherapy setting.

TONI: I fully agree that it isn't appropriate for a psychotherapist to work with a client on the illusion of a "separate me." This would just be working with an idea. As long as separation is felt to be a reality, "no-separation" remains an idea, a concept. The truth of what we really are, from moment to moment, can only be discovered in immediate insight. On an intellectual level, old ideas can be changed for new ones, but insight has nothing to do with exchanging ideas.

---

*skillfulness or wisdom in the choice of the means, or expedients for helping others

This chapter contains Toni's response to a letter from a retreatant. It was published in the Springwater Center Newsletter *of July 1993.*

Without calling it therapy or spiritual practice, we can explore our intense suffering together and alone when there is a deeply felt interest in questioning thoroughly what is going on in ourselves and in our relationship with each other. Genuine interest generates its own energy and inspires us to meet directly what is coming up mentally, emotionally, physically by listening and feeling quietly in a new way. This may hold for any one of us regardless of our particular psychological problems, which we all share to one degree or another. Disturbing emotional or behavioral symptoms do not necessarily prevent one from doing meditative work. And meditative work need not necessarily become an escape into stillness and a retreat from the pain and turmoil of psychological problems. As long as we genuinely need to find out what it is that is troubling us deeply, we can be increasingly present with whatever is going on in this troubled mindbody from moment to moment.

So why make any assumptions about what is or isn't possible for a particular person, including oneself? We really don't know, do we? Classifying ourselves according to our neurotic or psychotic symptoms and their prognoses, which is our usual approach to mental illness, does not help in this process, does it? The most amazing and seemingly improbable things are possible for a human being with an urge to grapple with fear, pain, and suffering without giving up, no matter how enormous the difficulty may appear to be. I don't know why, but we *are* capable of delving directly into sickness and what is making us sick, without escaping, by listening inwardly, quietly, without knowing. This listening-presence in itself renews the energy to carry on in unfathomable ways.

Direct insight into what is troubling us happens entirely on its own, without any "doing" on our part. It has no system, no strategy, no division. It is healing.

As for working on Mu for ten years, does it really illumine much about the immense power of thought, memory, and imagination to create and maintain our sense of separation and suffering? Working on Mu can actually be used to repress fear and pain and sorrow. At the same time it strengthens the thought and image of a separate self capable of becoming an enlightened one at a future time. Working on Mu

can hook us into all our old patterns of striving to attain a desired re-
ward, craving for success while experiencing failure. It hides rather
than reveals the conditioning that is going on and has been going on in
this human mindbody for thousands of years.

To me, working together with people who seek help means giving
careful attention to what comes up from moment to moment. I would
put the highest priority on listening and looking openly together, and,
if the occasion arises, asking questions in a simple way, without knowing or searching for immediate answers or solutions—letting feelings,
emotions, questions, or comments arise and unfold in that quiet listening space of not knowing. Isn't the problem of our moment-to-moment
living our central spiritual question?

This does not imply any pressure to work on a "spiritual question."
Our problems need not be labelled or categorized. And if a client suffers
from guilt feelings over not being able to work on a "spiritual" level,
these feelings themselves can become the focus of listening and questioning.

While I was in Zen training many years ago, my teacher asked me
to counsel students on their personal problems. He believed, as had
his teachers before him, that the discussion of psychological problems
did not belong in meetings between teacher and student. According
to Zen tradition, these meetings are for spiritual practice only, not for
bringing up personal things, no matter how urgent or upsetting they
might be. I did not know how to "counsel" people, and I found no
help from any system. All that remained was listening carefully to
what the person was saying, just watching what was happening in
both of us without knowing ways, means, or solutions. For me counselling is entering empty-minded into what someone is conveying and
what is coming up in oneself at the same time. This is difficult because the mindbody is addicted to its ingrained programs: thinking
about solutions, trying to get rid of pain and suffering in oneself and
others, wanting to be a successful helper and knower with all the accompanying satisfactions. But occasionally listening together without
any conditioned interferences unfolds its own wondrous wisdom, expression, and compassion.

Again, I'm not advocating anything like "working on the illusion of the self." That's all idea. The very stress and worldly suffering you talk about bring us to serious questioning, and that stress and suffering need to be allowed to manifest, to unfold. They need to be listened to, felt wholly, and inquired into in spacious stillness—alone and together.

What shall we call this amazing process of learning, with its spontaneous insights into the truth of what we really are?

Bringing the Unseen to Light: Therapy and Awareness

Anything that helps to bring into the open what has been under cover is of value. But I have to watch whether I'm merely revising my image of myself, or whether there is direct insight into the image-making process.

KEVIN: As you seemed interested in the type of work that goes on in my sessions with a counsellor, I will share some of what has happened so far. Basically I ask what is bothering me and then when a description or answer comes, I ask the body if that is really it. Then I see if there is something behind that and so on until I identify the exact place where all the energy is locked up. Then I feel it (and breathe). At least this is more or less what happens. . . . Well, . . . it's no big deal. It's not necessarily going to lead to open, undivided awareness. The value of doing therapy might be that I have a chance to express verbally what is in the absolute scuzziest parts of my mind to someone who doesn't react judgmentally. There is a relief in that. But obviously it's just a temporary fix, because one builds up the tension again.

One other aspect of therapy has been that I have had a chance to see more clearly how much I censor out of my awareness. In other words, the way one instantly pushes thoughts or the reactions to thoughts out of the mindbody in order to continue to appear or feel attentive.

TONI: We need to go into this censoring of awareness, this pushing "thoughts or the reactions to thoughts out of the mindbody in order to continue to appear or feel attentive."

Why is there this need to feel or appear attentive, I wonder. Is it an addictive attachment to the idea of being a "good boy" or a "good girl"

Kevin Frank was on staff as assistant administrator and foreman during the founding and construction of the Springwater Center. These are his letters from January 1989 and Toni's commentary in a talk at Springwater. The text was published in the Springwater Center Newsletter *of July 1989.*

with the energizing boost that causes throughout the body? Is there a compulsive need to demonstrate to myself and to others how "attentive" I am because in meditative practices, being attentive has taken on such an important value? Can we look at all that? Can we not only *think* about it but actually *see* thoughts and images as they energize the physical organism in pleasant or unpleasant ways, and the attachment to these feelings?

Is it the way of "mindfulness training" to censor thoughts and reactions in order to remain attentive? Many people mention to me the habit of using meditation practices to suppress and control undesirable "distractions." In doing that, the division into "me," the controller, and the distractions I must control continues unconsciously and unquestioned. That isn't awareness, is it? It is a cover-up staged by self-images.

Can awareness throw light on so-called distractions when we are not labelling anything as "distracting," not suppressing anything by concentrating on "being attentive," but seeing whatever thoughts, attractions, resistances, tensions and feelings arise? Can we avoid opposing or fighting anything and simply look at everything that's unfolding, without choice or judgment?

Open awareness means there's no controller. With awareness inner commands like "Don't become distracted! Be attentive!" reveal themselves. Valued images of being "good" and "attentive" are seen and felt to be connected with good feelings and with wanting—wanting to continue feeling good in one's own image and in the eyes of the imagined "others."

Can all this become transparent in the stillness and gentleness of no judging? We are not pushing anything away but watching the whole process of thinking, feeling, and wanting unfold without trying to stop it.

KEVIN: It is nice to just observe over and over and over the idiocy of the self and not defend it, not modify it, not dress it up for show. Yet I do continue to dress it up sometimes. I find it helpful to talk with other people about this. It is truly a passion to unmask the self, to see it naked, with whomever is interested in looking. Can one get attached to being a self-exposing zealot?

TONI: Yes. Yet even a self-exposing zealot may remain unaware of the subtle movements of the self, not only ignoring what is too threatening to look at, but also being unaware of becoming attached to a new identity as a self-exposer! What is the self?

We try to be something, become something, with almost everything we do. Isn't there a continuous creating or re-creating of images about oneself as somebody who is doing well or not doing well, someone who is worthy or unworthy of approval and love? This is happening all the time unless there is insight that detects and weakens attachment to pictures and ideas about ourselves.

We realize how the self-image nourishes the sense of "me" in a pleasurable way and at the same time hides the fact that the self-image is the cause of narrowness, isolation, and conflict. So when one sees the self-images of being "attentive or inattentive," and the attendant good and bad feelings, do those feelings lose power at the moment of seeing? When a self-image manifests at times of inattention, will it take complete possession of mind and body or won't it?

KEVIN: Recently, during a counselling session that my friend attended, too, I said some blunt things to her, arising out of things that I never get a chance to see in myself because they get censored because I am afraid of hurting her, or because her reaction comes before I really see what I am feeling. *Does it matter if we see what we are feeling?* Or is seeing what we are feeling too far away from seeing the "me"? It seems that seeing the "me" in action is a relief in and of itself. It's so laughable really. Why do I hold onto it if I really see what it is doing?

Can it be valuable to have a forum to blurt out the content of the "me's" complaints, so that they can be seen?

TONI: I'm looking. I know that one of the defense mechanisms of this organism is to shut down feelings when the idea of feeling hurt becomes too threatening and too painful. The mindbody becomes numb, thick-skinned, unfeeling. That may have happened early in life. But listening and attending inwardly, caringly, freely can actually dissolve the protective walls. Once self-protective walls begin to melt down, there is feeling again.

But I can very much get caught up in what my feelings are, how I am feeling at each moment. This is thinking about feelings. It's not direct feeling. It is a commentary. It's the same thing as thinking, "Now I'm attentive," "Now I'm feeling this way and that way," and becoming very important and interesting to myself and others by thinking about all the things I feel. Can there be simple awareness of what's going on without making something out of it?

You ask if it matters if we see what we are feeling. *All seeing matters*. Not just seeing feelings, but seeing their total interconnectedness with *thought*. Can there be a clear realization that the seemingly solid feeling of the self, the "me," to which there is such a powerful attachment, is an ongoing process of interconnected thoughts, feelings, emotions, and physical sensations, all rooted in memory?

You questioned whether it is valuable to have a forum for blurting out something one has never really seen before. *Anything* that helps to bring into the open what has been under cover is of value. But I have to watch whether I'm merely revising my *image* of myself, or whether there is direct *insight* into the image-making process.

Expressing to myself and to others what I am feeling easily adds to the "collected works" about myself, which continues to strengthen the sense of self, of "me." It's very rewarding to talk about myself, and to arouse someone else's interest in myself. We are deeply attached to the story of our life and love rereading it and adding new material to it. Isn't our life story one of our most treasured possessions, one that we valiantly pro- tect? Can we watch all of this very carefully, learning about ourselves in all simplicity without accumulating and without holding on?

KEVIN: I have been sitting [in meditation] and wondering formally for perhaps twenty years of my life. I spent at least fifteen of those years not seeing that my subtle grasping at a method was a trap. I spent many of those years struggling with pain in the body while sitting, thoughts about my inability to do what others seemed to be able to do, and so on. What a silly struggle. Now there are times of connectedness, of some degree of attention, some interruption of the "me's" shenani- gans. Krishnamurti would say that if the "me" is really seen, it ends for good. So something is not being seen.

TONI: Let's beware of recalling Krishnamurti's or anyone's words, because comparing one's momentary state of being with what Krishnamurti has said creates a new and unnecessary conflict. Can the clarity of seeing *now* expose the self-image without there being the expectation that it will be finished *once and for all*? Expectation is thinking, and that creates time. "Forever" is a concept of an infinite future. Direct insight into thought does not involve time—it's now!

You say, "So something is not being seen." That's clear. The sense of "me" is at the center of our whole *conditioned* consciousness. When the "me" is there, there is no seeing. Why does the "me" keep creeping up time and time again, even if it is clearly seen and dispelled for moments? Is this a thoroughly gripping question or just a casual musing? If it really is a serious question, there will be watching when self-images arise.

At a moment of insight one may be quickly sidetracked by powerful thoughts: "What will I become? Will I continue? Will I disappear? What will happen if there is really nothing? Will life be worth living without the 'me'?" None of these thoughts may be explicit, but they are there, moving murkily, creating anguish in their wake. Can they come to light while one is inquiring, whether alone or with someone else? Can one stop suppressing them as "distractions" and stop avoiding the fear that is generated in their wake, but rather be open to questioning, looking and listening without escape, come what may?

KEVIN: So something is not being seen. It's simple and it's clear. (Clear that it isn't clear.) One watches. There is still, after all these years, some eagerness in this lump of flesh. It is tremendously important to see the skipped spots in attention because in those there is some action of the "me," which is doing its merry damndest to survive and exist.

Okay. So one is looking, reaching into the corners of the closet. Now the question of the censoring of awareness comes in. Might not the joy of connectedness, the excitement and release of inquiry, be an intoxicating and potentially blinding factor? As one example, I, Kevin, come to see you, Toni, in a meeting. We grope for words to point at what the mind is itching to illuminate. We are good at that. There is a connectedness, a sense of no boundary, of flow, of movement in the mind. This is an alive place. There is some euphoria to it, not always, but frequently. Now this brain wants to search the corners for those sticky little pieces of no-looking that bring a narrowing down, a conflict, a sense of separation, and so on. In the act of merely looking at these items there is immediately a change in the whole texture of the mind. When there is this change, it is often a "no problem" state of the mind.

So my impulse lately has been to keep digging into the corners, deliberately, which is grasping. I'm not accepting that there is "no problem." Am I attached to the problems? Not really, just frustrated with how this person's grasping comes alive, is reborn over and over, despite its seeming to be gone completely at times.

TONI: Why do you want to dig into the dark corners of the mind deliberately if you realize that this itself is addictive grasping? Who is the digger, the grasper? What are the dark corners of the mind? When the grasping digger is illumined completely, are there any dark corners left?

KEVIN: Don't you get discouraged seeing friends sitting for years, moving with insight, and then somehow still getting trapped in the same shit as always?

TONI: Why waste time and energy on getting discouraged when we can look freshly, this instant?

KEVIN: So why this long abstract treatise? Is there perhaps a place for exposing more of the "me"? In other words, is there a place for deliberately enumerating and expressing the most intimate details of my grasping, to you, to another, in the hope (a word that drips with grasping itself) that by putting the contents of the garage out on the lawn, some of this stuff will be seen, which tends to slip by despite sitting, and meeting, and the whole nine yards of meditative inquiry?

Well, you do encourage individuals to bring all this stuff out of the closet and look at it. The key question is, is there some aspect of working with you that secretly *discourages* bringing all the stuff out of the closet completely and honestly?

TONI: It's an important question to ask. Can you look for yourself without being influenced by Toni or anyone else? Is there some aspect in our working together that discourages bringing all of the stuff out of the closet completely and honestly?

KEVIN: Or is there some auxiliary process that might help flush out some of the stuff that is hiding?

TONI: Is there an auxiliary process to *attention*? No matter what process of inquiry we may be engaged in to get in touch with more and more of ourselves, if there isn't the immediacy of *attention*, direct *insight* this moment, we end up just *collecting* more *ideas* about ourselves. Insight is not a process. It's not dependent on anyone or anything. It is not knowing. It comes on its own, shedding light. It cannot be grasped or possessed. It's either there or it isn't.

KEVIN: Then the whole question of technique and method arises. If one employs a therapeutic or merely a facilitating communication technique, one-on-one or in a group, what is the motive behind that technique? Does the facilitator really have no agenda of his or her own? I doubt it.

But don't you slowly, inevitably, condition your "nonstudents" to question in the same way *you* do, Toni? This ceases to be real skeptical questioning like that which comes so naturally to you. It rather becomes a subtle method that works very well to open up connectedness to you when you are around, but it seems so often to become a kind of formula, a security blanket that may prevent one from cultivating open awareness inside and out in the course of one's own life.

TONI: What you are describing has to be watched with great care: whether we are merely adopting a new vocabulary, a verbal technique, or whether there is clear understanding with direct insight. There's nothing wrong with using the same vocabulary as Toni or anyone else as long as we are aware that the words describing something are not the actual fact. So we have to ask ourselves, are we just parroting someone else, imitating a way of questioning, or are we looking directly? Can we actually tell the difference?

When doubt comes up, why not talk directly to each other to clarify things? Why not ask, "What do you mean by what you're saying? Could you say some more? I really want to understand what you are saying." If we don't communicate directly with each other, images about "you" and "me" grow like choking weeds, preventing any kind of understanding. Do we see that? Can we both see the same thing clearly at the same moment—not having the same opinions, but seeing directly?

I'd like to hear more about this way of questioning that is "Toni's." Is it "Toni's" inquiry or is it all of ours?

KEVIN: You do encourage people to question all of it. But are they?

TONI: Are we? Are all of us, including Toni? We have to wonder seriously, not assuming anything. As soon as one wants something, the "me" is there riding in the saddle. It doesn't want to question anything; it just wants to continue riding, being "me": "Look at me!" or "Don't look at me!" Are we questioning the whole thing? Will there be a glimpse of awareness as one is busily trying to impress someone or withdraw from someone, craving flattery or nursing hurts? Will there be a spark of attention to set fire to this whole self-enclosure?

KEVIN: For me there are places where I must not be questioning. And I will try any way I can to uncover those places. The danger of "any way I can" is obviously that it may add to the "collected works" about oneself, as you put it. What I am saying is that working in retreat with Toni may also add to the collected works. How can we bring that out of the closet?

TONI: This is what goes on: we find something out about ourselves, think about it, analyze it, and derive pleasure and satisfaction from accumulating knowledge about ourselves. Can that whole process be brought out of the closet? Will we keep adding new images about ourselves to the collection—how well or poorly we are doing, how much we have suffered, how happy we could be, and keep hanging on to memories? Or can there be a complete shift, bringing to an end what seems to be an endless self-concern with endless strings of closets? Not "forever"—who can say that?—but right now. It means not just seeing all the stuff in oneself, but *the ending of stuff* with nothing left to collect—no collector and no stuff. There are no closets to clean out because there are no closets when there's no collector. Is that clear?

KEVIN: How can the joy of working with Toni, in whose mere presence I feel there is no problem usually, be opened up deliberately to expose the hidden, yet-to-be-revealed stuck places?

TONI: What's hidden? Is one attached to Toni, wanting to be in her presence, wanting to please her, wanting her to smile upon one approvingly, lovingly? Sometimes we hug after a meeting, sometimes not. Does that create new images? Can one look at what happens immediately, deleting new images about me and you? Images do come up about "you" and "me"—that's been happening for thousands of years—but they needn't remain hidden. They can be seen coming and going. Then they don't narrow down the mind, divide it up, and create isolation and conflict.

KEVIN: Now if I go to a counsellor or some therapist who encourages me to spit out the unexpressed, the seemingly inconsequential, the associations, and so on, it's possible that I may say aloud something I never realized I was saying silently to myself.

TONI: Can we hear ourselves say something that has been going on implicitly, silently held inside? And with saying it out loud, is there genuine insight into what has been hidden, disguised, or ignored? We do talk to ourselves silently all the time, monologuing, dialoguing, arguing, with little or no real awareness. Can there be a fine tuning in?

There can be inner transparency. No one doing it, just the dawning of undivided awareness without judgment. It's not necessarily dependent on talking out loud in someone else's presence, even though that may help in uncovering what is hidden. Hearing and seeing hidden thoughts and feelings can happen in complete silence, when no one else is around. That's the amazing thing. Awareness simply reveals what was and what is.

KEVIN: It's taken me so long to be able to be honest about my not seeing and to admit that this is the entry point. That's the beauty of it. That is what I am wondering about. How can one encourage open inquiry into not seeing—inside and outside? Can one see the folly of appearing or acting as though there's no problem?

Is this silly, all this babble?

Today I sat, and then I skied across the lake and through the woods. The sound of the skis, and the blue sky, and the weeds sticking out of the snow, the lofty trunks of the pine trees were not of right and wrong.

Continuing the Dialogue: Defenses and Awareness

There's joy and great relief in being able to clearly see one's mistake and admit it freely, not as a new defense, but freely.

TONI: Kevin, in your letter you brought up some questions that would be interesting to discuss further. This is what you wrote: "Is there some aspect of working with you that secretly discourages the bringing of all this stuff out of the closet completely, honestly?" and "Is there some auxiliary process that might help flush out some of the stuff that is hiding?" Do you want to talk about that?

KEVIN: Yes. I'm not sure that there is anything in working with you that's secretly discouraging people from bringing things out of the closet, except all the conditioning that *I* have as a human being to not bring things out of the closet. I'd rather keep it all secret in order to . . . well, because I want things. I'm worried that if I bring everything out in the open, it will be dangerous to me.

In my relationships with different women who have been friends with me, I've often been told that I'm not aware of my real feelings. Or when I'm around certain other people, my feelings never come out. I never seem to have any problems. It's always the other people who end up talking about *their* problems. I have discovered I have had an image of being someone who is relatively free of problems.

Now I don't think there's anything about Springwater or about working with you that gave me that image of having no problems. When we question things very deeply together, you and I, oftentimes

---

This conversation between Kevin Frank and Toni and Kyle Packer followed the preceding letter and commentary. The meeting took place in New Hampshire in March 1989. The dialogue was published in the Springwater Center Newsletter *of October 1989.*

the questioning seems to lead to this relatively problemless state, a state of spaciousness, openness, of being in touch, especially in retreat. That's clear so far, what I'm saying?

TONI: Yes.

KEVIN: Let's say a former girlfriend says to me, "It was tremendously painful, what you did to me." What has become second nature for me is to listen to that and feel the discomfort of the negative image that arises when I hear those words. If I'm not able to do that, I may be defensive and come back with a reaction, trying to explain, "Well, I really didn't mean to hurt you," and so on.

In retreat or in meetings with you, when there's a problem, I've gotten used to questioning it. In other words, it feels as though the safest place to be is opening up the problem, sitting with it [meditating on it] or questioning it, embracing the feeling it creates in the body. The problem, during sitting, seems to dissolve. If I feel something completely, it does seem to abate or dissolve, so it almost becomes second nature to do that with whatever comes up as a problem.

TONI: In retreat.

KEVIN: Or out of retreat. But what concerns me is that sitting is sort of trying to let go of reacting, and to just feel what is going on in the body—to observe it and feel it. There's a directness in that. It doesn't really get into content. But it's not really listening to the emotions and knee-jerk reactions that come up in the mind when someone accuses me of doing something. I'm on the telephone and trying to process, to sort of digest the impact of what the other person is saying.

TONI: But the topic of the conversation is about what you did in the past?

KEVIN: Yes, yes, right. Right. The topic is trying to push me into memory. It evokes memory.

TONI: And that brings up the feelings that go with the memory, and being with that. But are you saying, "With all of that I may be free of the obstructions at this moment, with feeling bad . . . I may free myself"?

KEVIN: Yes, but I may have avoided the issue.

TONI: The issue being what?

KEVIN: I'm not sure.

TONI: How you're relating with another person, a woman, say . . . ?

KEVIN: Yes.

TONI: Or anyone, from moment to moment, right then.

KEVIN: Yes. I may go "out of relationship" in my attempt to deal with . . .

TONI: The aftereffect of what happened.

KEVIN: Yes.

TONI: And maybe while listening inwardly you can be free of the aftereffects because there is in-touchness with stillness and quietness now. Is there no carryover when you're again with your friend?

KEVIN: It feels as though that becomes a defense. You see, I question whether there really is openness. There may have been openness in retreat or at times, but then at other times it's not really openness. It's more of a defense. The ultimate defense is "to become one with the situation" [*laughs*] so to speak.

TONI: "Being one with the situation" in a narrow way.

KEVIN: Yeah, yeah. So I've been trying to climb out of that defense, trying to expose it, trying to catch it.

TONI: And what will shed light on all of that, so that it's not a partial openness, not just a partial awareness at the moment of interaction? It is clear that during retreat, when we're not interrelating in the usual way with each other, a direct problem about relationship seldom comes up unless relationship is reflected upon as memory.

KEVIN: Uh-huh.

TONI: So one has to ask whether in retreat there are also the defensive strategies and unnoticed self-images.

KEVIN: Yes, certainly . . .

TONI: Being "the attentive one."

KEVIN: "The attentive one!" There are all the images, all the fears held over from previous Zen training and so on. One is conditioned by being encouraged to stay focused, to stay clear, not to let up for one moment.

TONI: Not to get "distracted."

KEVIN: And also to really perform in a certain way.

Also, is one trying to make the work into a method? Is there an effort to know what one is doing? Do my questions come out of this reversion into "Can I find a way to ensure seeing? Can I find a way of applying this work as a method when I'm in conversation with someone and I feel I get stuck?"

TONI: What will bring awareness?

KEVIN: Yeah, that is the question: "What will bring about this awareness?"

TONI: Awareness. Complete awareness, not partial attention. Not "I must become one with the situation."

KEVIN: No.

TONI: Because in this idea of "becoming one with the situation," there is "me" needing to become one with "you" or the situation, and therefore there is a continuation of duality with its effort and conflict.

[*Pause*]

KEVIN: When you ask the question "What will bring about this awareness?" the mind immediately tries to supply an answer to that, [*laughs*] right? There's an impulse to say, "Yeah, what would do that?"

TONI: It's clear that unless awareness is there, patterned behavior repeats itself. Maybe a new pattern is substituted for an old one. One may have learned something and now intends to act differently by training oneself.

Let me go back to something you said earlier. You were saying that during retreat there may be in-touchness with stillness, spaciousness that dissolves the problem.

KEVIN: Especially in meetings. There's something about being in meeting with you that feels as though attention happens relatively effortlessly.

TONI: And that doesn't happen outside of meetings? Let's remain with retreat for the moment. There is an in-touchness—not "I'm in touch with it," but space and quietness, and everything and everyone participating in that. Does that happen only in meetings, or does it also take place at other times during retreat?

KEVIN: It happens also at other times, but there's something about being in a meeting when there's some recognition of what the mind state is. [*Laughs.*] At other times there may not be a lot of memory of spaciousness. . . . From moment to moment things are changing. . . . There are thoughts, . . . and then at breakfast there's just the spoonful of honey-swirled yogurt, the swallowing down the throat, the smell of earth coming in the springtime. . . .

TONI: And that doesn't have a partialness or a narrowness, does it?

KEVIN: It doesn't feel partial at all.

TONI: Why not? If we look at that moment, what is it about the quality of that moment, the spoonful of honey-swirled yogurt, the fragrance of wet earth? What is it?

KEVIN: It's unspoiled by the fear or wanting of "me."

TONI: Yeah. Unspoiled and not cut up by that. Not narrowed down by the wanting or the fearing of "me."

Now can a moment of being with someone outside of retreat, can that be like a meeting?

KEVIN: Yes. That happens. I'm speaking out of memory here, but it happens. And then there are times when suddenly it's a big mess. [*Laughs.*]

TONI: Yes. A big mess starts when—

KEVIN: When the wanting and the fearing of the "me" are evoked.

TONI: And they totally take over. Then there's—

KEVIN: Stuff!

TONI: There's no attention.

KEVIN: Yeah.

TONI: I think we're clear.

KEVIN: Yes, yes. It's again just the "me" trying to clear out the "me" here! Maybe all of those words that I wrote* are this ambition to make the joy of meeting with people into the pleasure of always being able to . . .

TONI: To have that.

KEVIN: To have that. To have that.

TONI: To be "me-less."

KEVIN: In other words, I make the joy of "me-lessness" into a memory, which becomes the "me." [*Laughs.*]

---
see previous chapter

TONI: Yes. There is the striving and the perpetuation of the "me"! And as that happens, as this process is going on, can that be seen? Can that be clear?

KEVIN: It feels like this is clarified.

TONI: Yes. Being methodless, being really unarmed.

KEVIN: Yeah, and not being unarmed in order to reproduce the state of unarmedness! [*Laughs.*]

TONI: No, no. That's all more of the shenanigans, more image building, and wanting and trying to attain something for oneself.

KEVIN: And I think this effort on my behalf of trying to do some counselling, some co-counselling, some sort of "true-confessions work," is an effort on the part of the "me" to maybe do some kind of—atonement? Some kind of protest and confession to the world. Which is defense! [*Laughs.*] So in this case nondefensiveness becomes a defense!

TONI: Yes! Yes, that's what you mentioned earlier. We corresponded about this: "Can one become a 'self-exposing zealot?'"

KEVIN: Yes.

TONI: Very much admired for one's courage and honesty, for putting it all out on the line. And in that there's a new image for "me": "Now I'm courageous and honest!"

KEVIN: Well, if there is some degree of awareness, that image-making can be recognized as a narrowing down. The whole space feels relatively claustrophobic all of a sudden because I'm focused on some kind of a goal.

TONI: Which doesn't mean there isn't a place for saying, "Yes, I really did that," to admit it openly, to be honest about it. But there's no need to make anything out of it, to become somebody in the process, using it for a purpose.

KEVIN: Then it's like entertainment.

TONI: Because sometimes self-exposing is not called for. It all depends. One can see whether it's appropriate or not, whether it really clarifies our relationship with each other or just adds more to the idea and image of "me."

There's joy and great relief in being able to clearly see one's mistake and admit it freely, not as a new defense, but freely. It is entirely possible to do that. It's totally survivable. We're so deathly afraid of it, but actually it's so easy. One does not get crushed in the process.

KEVIN: Yes. It is experiencing, maybe for the first time, that everything dreadful that one expected is in fact not the case, that all the fear that immobilized one was groundless somehow.

TONI: As children, in Germany, when, after having been forewarned, we did something clumsy like breaking a dish or spilling a drink, there inevitably came the scornful reprimand from the grownup: "*Siehste!*"—meaning "See, I told you so!" How we hated that word "*siehste*"! It felt so humiliating that we'd rather cover up what we did or blame it on something else than be shamed. To a child this is humiliating and painful, but we still carry this reactiveness to criticism even though we're no longer small children surrounded by all-powerful adults. But we can be freely aware of all of this, every pore of the body open and undefended, listening vulnerably in the presence of somebody saying "*Siehste!*" when we've messed something up—that's really marvelous! So much thick skin comes off, so much unnecessary armor.

KEVIN: The burden.

TONI: The burden, the weight of it.

KEVIN: What was the second question you brought up?

TONI: It was: "Is there some auxiliary process that might help flush out some of the stuff that is hiding?"

KEVIN: I think it depends. As you have pointed out, and as we have discussed this weekend, there are so many ways in which any process at all—why call it auxiliary—can be a way of creating a new existence for the "me."

TONI: Oh. What are you saying there?

KEVIN: Any type of discussion forum, any type of group meeting, any type of dialogue or psychological process or counselling can be a way to become more interesting to oneself. At the same time that I'm exposing things there is [*pause*], as you said, a new suit of clothes to put on.

TONI: And yet having a discussion, or counselling, or whatever one is doing, can that flush out some of the stuff that is hiding? What is the "flushing out"?

KEVIN: Well, the concern about what's going on.

TONI: And why would one be concerned?

KEVIN: Because there is a degree of chaos happening in my life—suddenly feeling the "me," usually the pain of the "me," rather than the pleasure of the "me." Oftentimes the pleasure of "me" gets by. The narrowness of the pleasure may get by. Obviously, the more I am aware of the narrowness of the pleasure as well as the pain of the narrowness of "me," the better it can be recognized.

TONI: But becoming aware of chaos in one's life can become a motive for wanting to flush out this stuff. And that again can be a narrow concern. . . .

KEVIN: Just to make my life less chaotic.

TONI: I don't want to have all these headaches and hangovers of feeling guilty afterward over what I did to someone. This can also be illuminated as there is an increasing concern over how we affect each other. Or one may not really be that concerned over how one affects someone else. . . . I don't know.

KEVIN: Ah. That may be something that needs to be flushed out: the relative lack of concern over how one affects others as opposed to how one deals with the chaos of one's own fortress.

TONI: Yes.

KEVIN: That may be something that would be pointed out to me, for instance, in a forum like counselling: "I see you doing a marvelous job of revealing the chaos of your own little Machiavellian brain, but what about all the chaos that is created in your wake?"

Now I had wondered whether there was some forum or process or counselling where one would be encouraged to do true confessions not for the sake of becoming a good confessor, but maybe to perceive that one could survive the letting down of some of that defensiveness. Just like you said, it's a marvelous thing to find that one can survive the "See, I told you so!" Suddenly one realizes it is survivable, not in terms of the "me" surviving, but—

TONI: Yes, that's a good point! We're not talking about the "me" surviving, but seeing through that feeling of doom that a little child has in being shamed or punished.

KEVIN: That hangs over our head for the rest of our lives unless there's a point at which I see this is a lie. It's not a dangerous thing! In fact, the dangerous things are all my defensive reactions trying to prevent the "I told you so" from ever happening again. So is there some way we can work together as people, one-on-one or in a group, assisting each other in the process of realizing that we are carrying a burden from the past?

Now when I say "some way," it implies a method or a formula for doing that. I don't think I mean that, but I'm wondering whether there is a situation that lends availability to that process of realizing, just as in retreat one makes oneself more available to a quieting-down and a coming-upon-seeing-something. Do you see what I mean? There's a difference between a method to get something, and some situation I would put myself in . . .

[*Pause.*]

TONI: For what?

[*Pause.*]

KEVIN: Well, maybe not "For what?" but because we're both concerned. We both have some mutual recognition that we as people are creating chaos in each other's lives.

KYLE: But unless the root cause of the chaos is seen, I don't know that anything else would work.

KEVIN: Yes, yes.

KYLE: Which means that the ultimate problem of the "me" has to be worked on.

KEVIN: Yes.

TONI: There's a very, very delicate line, a sort of razor's edge: where is the "me" being reborn, strengthened, or denied, and where is it simply being exposed, being seen directly for what it is?

[*Pause.*]

KEVIN: I think that very succinctly underlines the problem.

TONI: So can there be awareness of surreptitiously garnering support for "me"?

KEVIN: Yes. I think this is very good. You've hit upon precisely the right question.

TONI: Last night in our discussion, your friend said something that was really a very astute observation about thought always trying to arrest something that's flowing. I don't know if you recall it. She was really grappling with this, and you said, "Now that was a very good observation."

KEVIN: Yes. That's like giving a child in school a star for a good answer.

TONI: Exactly, exactly.

KEVIN: I saw that. It was very clear.

TONI: And she was not thrown off. [*Laughter.*]

KEVIN: She didn't lose it.

TONI: No, she didn't. Now I'm not trying to say what people should do in therapy or counselling, but rewarding each other while inquiring together can throw you off track.

KEVIN: Yeah. [*Laughs.*] No need to say, "You are doing a good job."

TONI: This doesn't mean one should never praise or criticize anybody. Just as one needs to find out that one can live freely with someone who says, "See, I told you so," listening openly and not being hurt or damaged, can one also hear someone say, "That was a good observation you made"? Is it possible to hear that (you actually feel good about it) yet not garner "me-support" from it? So when the "me" gets a boost, can one see it and feel it immediately, keep watching it, and not keep milking it endlessly?

KEVIN: Just feel the reverberations that have already been triggered in the body.

TONI: Feel that freely, yes, so that one is in touch with what's going on inside and out when one is either blamed or praised. It doesn't remain an abstract thing, but one clearly sees and feels what is happening, how one wants to continue with the good feelings and get away from the pain or shame. If one thoroughly sees and feels and listens to blame and praise, it cannot do damage. If a hurt occurs, or a flattery, neither need be milked. Neither need be carried over. The whole thing can drop lightly on its own. There need be no conscious intention to do so. It happens when there's pure seeing that is wisdom.

Religious Emotions

When there is no sense of self, is there religious emotion? When the self is not operating, religious experience takes on an altogether different meaning. Then it is the instant gathering of energy in the full presence of what is.

Dear Toni,

I teach religious studies and philosophy courses at a small Catholic liberal arts college.

I once set great store by religious emotion (as showing the cracking of the self, say, or as perhaps indicating small revelations). But I have found that sitting [meditation] tends to dissolve certain kinds of religious emotion. Is this the way awareness works? For example, last spring when I was teaching about Judaism and the Holocaust I found myself very nearly choking up in class. This fall I experienced something similar: tears at the thought of the Holocaust, inability to speak about it without tears welling up, and so on. I thought I would bring this matter to sitting. I basically found that if I was silent, the feeling didn't emerge. It is as if the feeling is tied to the verbalizing, so I am beginning to think that the "self" is itself also very much tied to verbalizing—almost as if the self were essentially a verbal activity. Much religious spiritual language then must itself be a kind of subtle self-activity.

Should this be so, my previous high evaluation of emotionality as revealing divine matters (I'm writing this a little tongue-in-cheek, but it has been a serious concern of mine) would actually be a subtle valuing of the self by the self, which could be of some temporary use, but in the long run it would be a delusion.

This chapter contains Toni's response to a November 1989 letter from a retreatant. It was published in the Springwater Center Newsletter *of October 1991.*

It is fortunate that you are able to go to Germany. The world is full of "Berlin Walls," isn't it—both inside and out?

Dear ———,

You write: "I have found that sitting tends to dissolve certain kinds of religious emotion. Is this the way awareness works?"

When one is sitting quietly with an open and aware mind and body, there is a diminution of disturbance through thoughts. Thoughts, if perceived immediately and fully, do not have the time to hook into further words and images, which are in turn linked with the emotion-arousing system of the organism. This can be directly observed.

Your question whether the self is essentially a verbal activity is well worth pursuing. It is clear that there is no such thing as pure verbal activity. Words are linked to remembrances, and remembrances have links with the emotions, feelings, and sensations that were present at the time of the remembered experience. All of this is called up instantly with a present thought or word or feeling. It can be seen freshly time and time again. In our daily way of living, words do seem to lead the way though, don't they?

And is much religious, spiritual language itself a kind of subtle self-activity, you ask. Let's question it thoroughly by examining what is observed directly in ourselves and in others. We are identified with our religious thoughts, experiences, and emotions, aren't we? These are felt to be a highly valued part of "me," I defend them if they are attacked. What remains of the self when thoughts and words with all their associated emotions and sentiments are seen through in quiet listening?

When there is no sense of self, is there religious emotion? When the self is not operating, religious experience takes on an altogether different meaning. Then it is the instant gathering of energy in the full presence of what is.

We think/feel that strong emotions experienced during church services or other religious rituals and ceremonies give evidence of the workings of the Divine. Who is it that thinks that? Who feels that? Who has invented the ceremonies and Scriptures in the first place and then feels divinely inspired by them? One may protest that these are the words and revelations of the Divinity, but our protestations do not turn conviction into truth.

Could emotionality actually be "a subtle valuing of the self by the self," you are wondering. Can one have direct insight into this as it happens and not be deluded? Can delusion end in immediate perception?

You write in your letter about experiencing choking emotions when talking and thinking about the Holocaust, yet no feeling emerged when you sat quietly with the matter. Can we look at that more closely? One must be careful not to dismiss or suppress emotions, or maybe rationalize their absence by thinking that the self has actually quieted down. In investigating anything, can one start from scratch, observing carefully and deeply what is actually happening?

What emotions come up in thinking and talking about the Holocaust? Do thoughts and images bring up anger, thirst for vengeance, painful sadness and pity, horror and revulsion, fear and anxiety, as well as guilt and shame about what went on? All of that can arise at the thought of the Holocaust. And not thinking about it and thereby avoiding the turmoil of emotions does not necessarily mean that the whole problem has been understood on the deepest level. What does it mean to understand a problem on the deepest level? We don't know, but maybe we can find out.

Is it possible to examine all one knows about the Holocaust freshly, without previous judgment? Further, can one wonder about what went on in the minds of human beings to be able to conceive of all that they were doing—organizing it, executing it, and living with it? And can one look into oneself to see where such potential originates, while watching closely and carefully one's moment-to-moment thoughts and reactions? Can all this inward questioning, looking, and listening take place in the stillness of taking no position, making no opposition, just seeing and feeling the immense tragedy and sorrow of human ignorance with its chaotic consequences? Can there be just the utter silence of what is and what has been? In such stillness there may be the dissolution of division and separation, and the emergence of compassion.

The Berlin Wall has come down since you wrote. But are we bursting into real freedom by exuberantly smashing a cement wall? True freedom is freedom from all emotional identification with a nation, a race, an ethnic group, a religious creed, an ideology—freedom from attachment to a self that has constant demands and is constantly in fear. Is the coming down of the Berlin Wall a first step toward this freedom? I don't know. The invisible wall is the one we take utterly for granted—the wall around the idea of "myself" and the "others" out there. Can it become visible and come down?

Religious Institutions

Is the insight that religious institutions create division enough to end this division in oneself? Does seeing one's attachment to the institution end the attachment?

Dear Toni———

Religious and other social institutions designed to encourage or rediscover harmony often only succeed in doing the opposite: creating more division and encouraging men and women to distrust the authority of their own experience. This I understand to be one of your points. The way I understand it, it's virtually impossible for something to be inherently good or bad, but it is only made so by the judgment of human beings.

It seems to me that the religions and institutions within our minds need to be examined, but that the external ones cannot be avoided. Men and women live in a relative world. They speak a certain language yet need not be imprisoned by it. They have certain preferences yet need not be caught up in them. I wouldn't say that being outside a specific religious tradition is "wrong," but perhaps it is impossible. Even the attitude of "all religions are obstacles" is an obstacle for which people would kill and die (and have). I think you must agree, but please tell me if you think I've ignored something.

Dear ———

It is crucial that we see what is judgment or opinion and what is a fact. When you say, "Religious and other social institutions designed to encourage or rediscover harmony often only succeed in doing the opposite:

This chapter contains Toni's response to a May 1991 letter. It was published in the Springwater Center Newsletter *of January 1992.*

creating more division," is that a judgment, or is it a fact? To clearly see a fact for what it is, is enough, isn't it? Judgment is extra and detracts from the clarity of insight into a fact.

Is the insight that religious institutions create division enough to *end* this division in oneself? Does seeing one's attachment to the institution end the attachment? Does seeing one's identification with the institution end the identification?

Why are you differentiating between internal and external religious institutions? Don't both arise mutually? How can one be separated from the other? Our religious institutions, having become part of our internal conditioning, have also become our attachment, and our attachment keeps the religious institutions going.

You say that external religions and institutions cannot be avoided. It's true: they are there. But can *attachment* to a religious institution be seen intelligently and wither away in the seeing? We are all programmed. We cannot avoid that. But insight into one's own programming comes from no program. Insight has its own intelligent action.

Is being outside a religious tradition impossible? This is nothing to speculate about, but one can experiment if one is really curious, deeply interested in whether a human being can stand on his or her own without the intervention of, and attachment to, a religious tradition.

If the attitude "all religions are obstacles" becomes *dogma*, then we will kill and die for it as we would for any dogma we are identified with and therefore feel compelled to defend. Understanding that all dogma is an obstacle to clear seeing, will the attachment to it drop away on its own?

Schooling

*No school teaches children, parents, and teachers about that—
how we are constantly programmed to think in fixed categories
about what we are, and what we should be like, and to see for
ourselves the way these programs affect our present thinking,
feelings, and performance.*

Dear Toni,

Today is the first day of school, and, as on previous first days, I find myself asking whether or not public school is really what I want for the
children. Ideas for an alternative have been tumbling through my head.
I've done some reading, some talking with people, and had discussions
with my son and my husband, hoping to gather enough information to
make an informed decision. More than once I have heard you mention
the subject of education in your talks, and I thought that either you or
your husband might be willing to share your observations with me.

Ours is one of the better public elementary schools in the county, but
it is not so good that I can feel easy about our son's continuing there—
third grade this year. Our daughter will be in kindergarten and is not
so much affected by all this.

Our son has gone from being an enthusiastic student who refused to
stay home from school even when ill to a child who sometimes whines,
cries, screams, begs, and even gets an upset stomach before school, in
anticipation of the day to come. When asked what he dislikes about
school, he says first that the day is too long, then that the work is boring, and finally that he doesn't like timed math tests. This last comment
correlates with his increasing fear of failure and his frustration with
any work that isn't easily accomplished. He's very sensitive to performance pressure. Simply opening his notebook to homework problems

---

*This chapter contains Toni's response to a September 1990 letter from a friend.
It was published in the* Springwater Center Newsletter *of January 1991.*

can bring on bursts of tears and cries of "I'll never be able to do all this!" (He always can.) He quit piano lessons when he reached a point where he had to work at the pieces rather than being able to play them quickly and easily. He signed up for the soccer team but then refused to go to practice. Something about commitment disturbs him.

Anyway, I have seen his excitement about learning transforming into fear and frustration. Even though he earns glowing report cards, the pressure he feels (at times) makes me uneasy. There are three possibilities of which I am aware: working with the public school teachers to make changes, switching to the sole private school in town (essentially an expensive public school with smaller classes, but that's an improvement), or homeschooling. I'm looking into all options. It doesn't feel right to send him off all day and get back a tired child for a few hours at night. When I consider homeschooling, I like the idea of autonomy fostered in a child who can share responsibility for his own education and have some control over the subject matter. On the other hand, schools have a lot of resources and teachers who can devote the entire day to teaching, neither of which I can offer here at home.

What I want for both children is a sense of independence, control, confidence in their abilities to learn, excitement about learning, and the belief that what they learn has relevance in their lives. (One of our son's comments, which occurred some time after one of our discussions about school, as though he'd been mulling it over and just couldn't figure it out, was "Why did all of us second-graders have to learn about penguins?")

I once mentioned the possibility of his attending the private school with its smaller classes and more student-guided study and found that he was interested. Then I brought up homeschooling. He looked up at me with a mixture of hope and disbelief: "You can't really do that, can you?" We discussed the idea and he would like very much to do it, but I think he sees it more as summer vacation than as a time for learning.

I had a conference with his teachers and took along a list of concerns that he had dictated to me. (Just knowing that these concerns would be aired relieved some of the stress he was experiencing: he had some power, some control over his life again.) His teachers were very much open to working with me to keep him involved and interested, within the confines of the required curriculum. The curriculum is the point of inflexibility. His teachers are excellent, warm women. They understand that he needs to feel safe with them, not defensive. They want to give him latitude to follow his interests, but they have to follow the curriculum, and there is testing to prove that the material has been adequately taught. I think this school system and these teachers are as good as any the public schools have to offer, but I'm still unconvinced that it's the best way for him to learn. But can I provide him with as many opportunities for learning? How much of what is taught at school does he really need to know? I don't know what the answer to all this education stuff is, but he trusts me to do my best for him.

Do I have faith in him, in his ability to follow his own interests and rekindle the joy of learning, without school? Do I give him this time to heal? Do I work with the teachers to give him the best they can offer, while supporting his individual efforts at home?

At every step of the path in caring for my children, from prenatal care through the present education situation, I have found myself at odds with mainstream thinking. I've never been sorry that I birthed them at home, nursed them for years, kept them in our bed at night, used cloth diapers, fed them vegetarian meals, restricted TV, and so on. You'd think I'd have some confidence in my gut feelings by now, but messing with their education is a big step. Can you offer any comments that might be helpful? Any thoughts will be appreciated.

Dear _____,

You have certainly made a careful and thorough examination of the whole problem, raised many important questions, and taken appropriate and significant actions. Rather than just looking for answers, can you also keep these questions alive, continuing to deepen your understanding of the problem? I don't really have anything to add to what you have already said about the options of homeschooling for your son, private school, or continued public school education in friendly cooperation with his teachers. Right now you seem to be experimenting with the latter in order to find out if it works out better for him.

Kyle, with all his school experience, says that he hasn't known a healthy child who wasn't basically interested in learning. Disturbances in learning are caused by the notions and anxieties the child has picked up about school and himself, and the blockages these produce throughout the brain and body.

You mention that your son quit piano lessons and soccer training because he was disturbed about commitment to practicing. Would it be possible to let a child *play* at these things more naturally rather than immediately organizing everything into a serious endeavor? A child may not grow up to be a virtuoso concert pianist or the most valuable soccer player, but he might have real fun in playing and, incidentally, learning, if adults allowed it to happen without pressure for results. As to the penguins . . . I wonder how penguins were "taught" to the kids. Did they have workbook pages to fill out about them? Did they have to answer test questions that were graded, write so many words about penguins as a "study project"? With that kind of treatment we usually manage to kill a child's original and spontaneous interest. At the zoo or in the country children usually watch animals with great interest and delight. What happened that turned these fascinating and playful birds into a problem?

Most schools work for speed in learning and toward more, rather than less, competitiveness among the children, and most parents want it that way because they want their child to come out on top, or at least in the top bracket. Who will have the concern or even the nerve to question competitiveness itself—the damage it does to us and to our relationship with each other? Competitiveness is one of the sacred values of our society, presumed to work all the wonders of growth and progress. But what is the price of this "growth and progress"? Can we see how caught up we are in these values ourselves? We are the society. Do we question these values thoroughly whenever we see them arise? Not immediately knowing the answer? We can see the seriousness of the problem manifesting in a frustrated child who gets an upset stomach before going to school, who is crying, screaming, begging not to go, thinking he will "never be able to do all this" even though he is capable.

These are the things I would ponder, look into a lot, and openly talk over with your son, if he is interested. I would start with his present concerns as he expresses them, listening carefully without immediately trying to find a solution, looking together, on the same level, at all the different ways in which we think about ourselves: "good" or "no-good" in math, "liked" or "not liked," by the teacher, "capable" or "incapable" of doing something—and the tremendous influence that these ideas and images about ourselves have on our feelings and on our performance. No school teaches children, parents, and teachers about that—how we are constantly programmed to think in fixed categories about what we are, and what we should be like, and to see for ourselves the way these programs affect our present thinking, feelings, and performance.

We see how deep a thorough questioning of education takes us. Are we interested in going that far, alone, and with our children?

You write that you have been at odds with mainstream thinking about caring for your children. It is worth noting that schools do not question the programming of children in matters of patriotism, going to war to fight for conditioned ideals or for self-centered interests. Schools are supposed to instill these ideals and the justification for taking whatever actions are deemed necessary for maintaining these ideals. Questioning all of this can only happen at home, or wherever we can sit down quietly, undisturbed, and look at it together in an atmosphere that is open and nonthreatening.

In case you haven't read any of Krishnamurti's books on education, I can highly recommend them.

Relationships in the Workplace

What happens when one is watching carefully, without judging, what goes on within oneself as one assigns work, points out mistakes, and reacts to other people's reactions? Can insight into all this purify action?

QUESTIONER: I am a manager of people, in a medical clinic, yet managing is the hardest thing for me to do. I am constantly afraid of telling others what to do. Therefore I find myself avoiding doing so, and that only makes matters worse. Questioning where this fear comes from, I see the desire to be liked, the fear of rejection, and the fear of failure.

I know I have lost the respect of my staff. They see the fear that I try so hard to avoid, to hide from. Facing the fear, and questioning what this fear is, helps. Yet on a day-to-day level, I see myself caught up and overwhelmed by feelings of inferiority and "should's" and wants. When I make a decision and act on it, I find the power within to face this fear and be the supervisor of people.

My workers are constantly testing me, trying to get away with coming in late, not doing the work they are supposed to do, treating patients terribly, and so on. I know their jobs are hard and the pay is little. Yet when I see the things that aren't getting done, I get angry, frustrated, and I lash out at myself and others at work. This just makes matters worse.

Please help me sort through all this.

TONI: One of the responsibilities of a supervisor is to maintain an orderly flow of work among people who have agreed to do that work. Asking people to do and not to do certain things is part of this responsibility.

This chapter contains Toni's response to a June 1985 letter from a friend. It first appeared in The Work of This Moment, Awareness in Daily Life, *in the edition published by the Springwater Center in 1988.*

You write that telling people what to do or not to do arouses fear in you—fear of being disliked for being bossy or critical and fear of failing in the job. On the other hand, *not* telling people what to do, or vacillating about it, creates disrespect among the staff as well as constant testing of "authority." What is one to do?

You mention that when you make a decision and act on it, you find the power to face fear and to function adequately as a supervisor. This means, doesn't it, that if one sees a situation not just from one's own personal vantage point of gaining or losing respect and approval, but also clearly, as a whole, then there is the energy to act appropriately. When a situation is seen impartially as a *whole*, one's own fears and apprehensions become simply one element of the whole thing. Then decisions needn't be distorted by the fear of personal consequences.

If fear is triggered, can it be faced immediately as it arises? Being directly, intimately, nonjudgmentally in touch with fear can open the way to right action. One can find this out for oneself.

Looking at this matter of supervision from a slightly different point of view, one may even question whether being a "strong supervisor" is an unequivocally "good" thing. It is a fact that we human beings often cease to think, inquire, and respond for ourselves when we have a strong supervisor in command. Do you have staff meetings in which specific questions of responsibility, and perhaps the whole matter of responsibility in general, can be brought up and discussed openly and freely? Can you talk together on an equal level, not as the manager with "his" or "her" staff, but on friendly ground so that you can shed light on your common inner processes?

For example, if a person comes in late but gets things done nevertheless, is lateness a real problem? It may be a problem if things have to be done together on time. It may become a problem if co-workers feel "If she or he comes in late, I can too." Coming in late may be a show of resistance, negligence, testing, or it may be owing to some personal circumstances at home or on the road. When one is given the space to see for oneself what each day, each moment demands, then symptoms like tardiness may not be a problem.

When we begin to feel responsible for what we are doing—not just working because a person in charge directs us, or because we get a paycheck for it, but because the need for the work is clearly obvious—there may be less need for supervision.

One more thing about the function of a supervisor. Can one watch very attentively to see if one is simply coordinating the flow of work (or whatever is involved with the work as such), or whether the position, power, and prestige that go with supervising are very important to oneself? Concern for the "respect" in which one is held can be a clue that the need for self-importance is operating. Can one honestly, carefully question and look at how self images are operating?

To the extent that the "me" is trying to establish and aggrandize itself, constant trouble lies ahead. Human beings do resist, in open and hidden ways, submitting to someone else's ego trips. So as a supervisor, one may worry about subjecting other people to the self's need to feel important and powerful (if one becomes aware one is doing that), and at the same time, one may feel anxious about losing face. Along with attaining and maintaining position and status always goes the fear of losing it, and of not "making good." Conflicts between guilt, desire, and fear add to inner stress.

What happens when one is watching carefully, without judging, what goes on within oneself as one assigns work, points out mistakes, and reacts to other people's reactions? Can insight into all this purify action? When the "me" in all its moment-to-moment manifestations is seen clearly, what happens to its controlling power? Can it abate?

When the "me" is in abeyance, the need for power and approval recedes. It is much easier to ask someone to do something when the "me" is not openly or subtly in charge. And similarly, the one who is asked to do something will find it easy to respond if he or she sees that the supervisor is not asking anything for him or herself.

Neither power, position, nor approval by "others" can make one feel secure. Security cannot be given by anyone or anything. Security ceases to be an issue when one does not want anything, and when one feels free to do what needs to be done. Then work may give rise to a joy that does not depend on anyone or anything. And the people one works with can be seen, maybe even affectionately, for what they are—not separate from oneself.

Motives for Performing

One has to look and find out for oneself whether performance (or whatever one may be doing) can happen entirely for its own sake, for the sheer love of doing it regardless of the results it may bring or fail to bring.

Dear Toni,

Can you help me with this? I am going to music school. I am also doing a lot of dancing and creative writing. On the first page of a journal I keep I have copied from your book the poem about sitting. Every few lines, I inserted the word "playing," because I also wanted this way of being to be as much a part of my music as possible. Tonight when I was reading it, the lines "attending and questioning thoroughly,/ not getting entangled in thoughts of attainment/ or fear of failure"* particularly stood out for me.

Lately I've been catching myself realizing that wanting to be the *best* is a large part of my drive to write and perform. I see that the fear of failure and the disappointment of not being the best can be almost paralyzing, and that they are also very selfish reasons to act or dance or write. I see this, but I don't know where to go from here.

How can I come to "better" motives for performing? For sharing my gift with others? I am not often enough that altruistic, "at one with others." From time to time I see that at some level there is no real separation between audience and performer, but not often enough. And when I sit and think about performances and reasons for performing, I

*in Seeing Without Knowing, *published by the Genesee Valley Zen Center in 1983*

This chapter contains Toni's response to a January 1985 letter from a friend. It first appeared in The Work of This Moment, Awareness in Daily Life, *in the edition published by the Springwater Center in 1988.*

have to wonder, why have any kind of performance or writing? For the audience's enjoyment? Can I perform without fear of failing and without wanting to get something in return?

Dear ————,

It is interesting that you are discovering different motives for performing, and that you are carefully watching ideas, feelings, and conflicts about wanting to succeed, wanting to be the BEST, and fearing failure. In seriously pondering one's motives for acting, one cannot help questioning: "Why perform or write at all?" or "Can I perform without the constant fear of failing or wanting to get something in return?" We'll go into those questions later.

First of all, can impartial observation, discovery, and questioning go on from moment to moment, empty of any assumption that one has gotten to know one's feelings and motives well enough and therefore needn't give them attention any longer? Past knowledge about oneself is just that: past. It is memory, conceptualization, and never the present living thing. Furthermore, a motive doesn't cease to function just because one has recognized that it was operating in the past. If inner awareness and attention aren't there, motives operate unconsciously and compulsively, perpetuating self-enclosure and conflict. So can simple, nonjudgmental awareness shed light on one's daily life without there being expectation of immediate tangible results?

You say that wanting to be the best is a selfish motive for acting, and you wonder if you can come to "better" motives. Before trying to come to "better" motives, can we look closely at the existing ones? What does it mean inwardly to want to be the best? It involves, doesn't it, an idea of perfection, perhaps the image of a great virtuoso. Trying to measure up to that image requires enormous ambition. That carries with it stressful side effects: strain, frustration, and maybe a growing callousness, envy, or jealousy toward people who get in one's way. Striving to attain perfection may result in great virtuosity, but it cannot accomplish a relationship of kindliness and care with the people around one. Rivalry and love do not exist side by side.

Wanting to be the best involves continual comparison of the present image of oneself with the ideal "self" one would like to become in the future. All of this is the activity of thinking. Comparison inevitably creates conflict: one often comes to hate one's present "imperfections." Conflict and dissatisfaction with the way one is prevent one from being in touch with what is actually happening in oneself and the people around one. Comparison makes clear perception impossible, for one is constantly stuck with feelings of superiority or inferiority. Do you see it like this too?

If one sees directly the distorting effect comparison has on perceptions, can it drop? What happens in a performance if one doesn't compare oneself with anyone? Maybe only then can one's voice, words, or movements begin to flow naturally, creatively. On the other hand, one may be afraid that without the spur of comparison one will not improve. We don't trust simple awareness to operate on its own, without the habitual imposition of models and standards.

Wanting to be the best, while promising the exhilaration of success and fame, inevitably produces the anxiety of failing—failing oneself, failing one's parents, teachers, friends, and the audience. The fear of disappointing others. The horror of making a fool of oneself. Again, self-images are at the root of this fear of failing: "What will I be in the eyes of others if I don't bring it off?" "Who will still love and admire me?" The *self*, with its vast array of images, is insatiable in its need for love and approval. It is also in constant need of repair and maintenance.

Is it the longing to be loved, admired, and thereby made "secure," that largely propels us to write and perform for an audience? Does our lack of love and stability drive us to seek reassurance through an audience? All of this can be questioned and looked into with care and honesty as one writes, rehearses, plays, and is received by the audience. There is no moment in life that isn't ripe for seeing and discarding images.

Let us return to the questions about why one would perform at all, and whether one can perform without any wanting or fearing. These questions cannot possibly be answered through intellectual speculation. One has to look and find out for oneself whether performance (or *whatever* one may be doing) can happen entirely for its own sake, for the sheer love of doing it regardless of the results it may bring or fail to bring.

Can one give one's total being to *whatever* one is doing at the moment yet have the space of awareness? If attention is operating non-judgmentally, then self-images of grandeur or inferiority can be seen and discarded naturally, because they simply get in the way.

If self-images are *not* noticed, performance becomes a vehicle for "self-expression" in which habitual desires, vanities, agonies, and fears take over the mindbody. Acting, writing, or playing become pure in the very process of seeing.

When *you* are not there, the "audience" isn't there either. Then, maybe, words, sounds, and movements are the unhindered flow of life itself.

Right Livelihood

*Whatever we may be doing during the twenty-four hours a day,
be it working for money or working for fun or service, whether
cleaning or just sitting quietly—the doing now, in this moment
of no separation, is the fulfillment, and it affects everyone and
everything everywhere.*

If we want to find out about right livelihood, where do we start? Without giving advice or answers, having no fixed point of view, no "good" ideas, no set of morals or religious precepts, we start with a blank page: We really don't know what "right livelihood" is. Can we question together without knowing?

A friend who has been concerned with the problem of right livelihood suggested many questions for this article:

What is helping (or helpful) work?

If I am independently wealthy, should I work? Should I "do my share" or "be of service"?

Is it important to find work that I enjoy? Work that allows me to use my "full potential"? How can I find such work?

Is it important to consider the impact of what I do on the world, on other people, on the ecology, on society, and so on? Are certain jobs morally or actually "bad" or "wrong"?

Is it okay *not* to use skills or talents one has? Or should they be put to use for the good of humanity?

Is it wrong to want money? Does "right livelihood" mean being involved in service work and not wanting money?

Could something frivolous or playful or beautiful be right livelihood?

Reprinted with some changes from "What Is Right Livelihood?" by Toni Packer in Mindfulness and Meaningful Work: Explorations in Right Livelihood, *edited by Claude Whitmyer (1994), with permission of Parallax Press, Berkeley, California.*

Does the advice to "follow your bliss" or "do what you love"
  mean anything? Is that good advice?
How do I figure out what to do with my life? I want to help
  people and use my skills and enjoy what I do. What should
  I do? Is what I'm doing enough?
Are moral guidelines or ideas important?
What is my responsibility to the poor and underprivileged? Do I
  have an obligation to use the "privileges" I have (money, edu-
  cation, class, health) to help others?
Is it possible to help others even though one is not totally free
  from conflict oneself?
What is creative work?

What are we going to do with all these different questions? Shall we
attempt to go through them one by one? Or can we just let them be
there without immediately trying to find answers?

Before seeking answers, can we look openly, quietly, inwardly, to
find out where our questions about right livelihood come from?

Perhaps they are coming out of a deep sense of separateness. Do I
feel that I am separate from society, separate from the privileged or the
underprivileged, separate from the world, from humanity, from the
environment? Do I feel that life itself is something separate, apart,
from me?

If the question "What is right livelihood?" arises out of my idea/feel-
ing of being a separate entity, doesn't it follow inevitably that I yearn for
a livelihood that will compensate me for what I feel lacking and hurting inside? That I will try to compensate for feelings of insecurity, lack,
discontent, guilt, loneliness, fear, and wanting through work that cov-
ers over these feelings?

Not being aware of what motivates my drives and ambitions, won't
I compulsively strive to possess people and things? Won't I strive for
power, position, fulfillment of my potential, bliss, enlightenment,
peace, or the humbleness of self-abnegation and service to others?

Am I driven to do something helpful for humanity or the endan-
gered planet because I feel achingly apart from everything? Do I expect

through my daily work to bridge the gulf of separation between me, humanity, and nature to bring about feelings of completion, of wholeness, of fulfillment? Can whatever work I'm doing really heal separation?

We need to go deeper. Can separation be healed? Maybe it needn't be healed at all. It may not be true! Is separation real or just a dream dreamt by human beings like you and me from time immemorial?

Can we wake up to the fact that separateness isn't real at all—that it exists only in thoughts, images, feelings? Are we interested in finding out the truth of this? Can we stop believing someone else's pronouncements or refuting them with argumentation and instead start inquiring patiently and deeply into this strong sense of "me," this "I" that feels so convincingly real and separate from everything else?

In truth we are not separate from each other, or from the world, from the whole earth, the sun or moon or billions of stars, not separate from the entire universe. Listening silently in quiet wonderment, without knowing anything, there is just one mysteriously palpitating aliveness.

When our habitual ideas and feelings of separation begin to abate in silent questioning, listening, and understanding, then right livelihood is no longer a problem. Whatever we may be doing during the twenty-four hours a day, be it working for money or working for fun or service, whether cleaning or just sitting quietly—the doing *now*, in this moment of no separation, is the fulfillment, and it affects everyone and everything everywhere. Everyone and everything is inextricably interweaving in this mysterious fabric called life. Can we not just understand this intellectually, theoretically, but experience it profoundly?

When we are not feeling separate from ourselves, cut off from each other, from the environment, and from life in general, but are deeply experiencing the togetherness of it all, we do not need moral guidelines or religious precepts to refrain from killing, or hurting, or blindly damaging the natural environment.

I see clearly that hurting you also hurts me as well as others. Caring for you, I care for myself. Attending to what I do, I also attend to you and to the earth on which we live.

Is what we call our full potential anything but being fully alive this very instant with all there is? Our "bliss" is living immediately, undefendedly, open . . . in touch.

Is this love?

Compassion and Impermanence

*How difficult it is to simply be with what is, . . .without all kinds
of thought programs taking over, without making a problem out
of it. Thoughts and reactions create moods and consistently
strengthen the sense of self. And from that center nothing can be
seen clearly, including the poverty surrounding one.*

Dear Toni,

We spent last January in India and Nepal—quite an experience. Nepal
is very, very beautiful, and I liked the people a lot. They are as poor as
the Indians, but so far they have retained more of a sense of identity and
pride. We spent a week on a lakeside retreat from which we could
watch the sunrise over the Himalayas. Gorgeous!

India was very difficult. We were in some of the poorest regions, and
there was an overwhelming sense of pollution, poverty, and disease. We
had, of course, expected to see poverty in India, and I have seen a fair
amount of it in this country, but nothing prepared us for the poverty in
India. The part that troubled me most was my reaction. Instead of feeling compassion, which would normally be my response, I felt revulsion. I felt genuinely guilty about this: it is hard to accept the fact that
after so many years of training, my sense of compassion could fail me so
utterly. What do you think causes this?

The other question that has been rattling around my head for a while
has to do with impermanence. It seems that I have a pretty fair grasp of
the transient nature of phenomena, but my reaction to it is strikingly var-
ied. On the one hand, I find impermanence a source of liberation and joy.
On the other hand, I find it distressing and depressing. These responses
seem to come in response to exactly the same set of stimuli, yet they are so
diametrically different. Do you have any thoughts on this?

---

*This chapter contains Toni's response to a June 1991 letter from a friend. It was
published in the* Springwater Center Newsletter *of January 1992.*

Dear ———,

I was interested in your description of experiencing revulsion where you had expected to feel compassion in seeing the poverty, pollution, and disease in India, and then feeling guilty about your failing sense of compassion. "What causes this?" you ask.

Revulsion is a conditioned reaction, isn't it? It is not simply experiencing directly what is there—seeing squalor, poverty, pollution for what they are and what they do to human beings. There is no one to fault in this reaction: it arises in brain and body just as any other learned or instinctual program does. The moment revulsion comes into awareness, however, another conditioned train of thought may take over: "How bad of me to feel revulsion when I should be compassionate. What's wrong with me? I wish I would have responded differently."

How difficult it is to simply be with what is, whatever it happens to be, without all kinds of thought programs taking over, without making a problem out of it. Thoughts and reactions create moods and consistently strengthen the sense of self. And from that center nothing can be seen clearly, including the poverty surrounding one.

Maybe compassion is not what we think it is. What is it? We may think of it as a feeling of deep sorrow for poor people, being merciful, having pity on them, wanting to do something for them, like praying or chanting, working to help, improve, or save them, or whatever. But where do these impulses come from? Do they spring from the clarity of this moment, or are they conditioned responses from a self-center that doesn't like to witness squalor, suffering, pain; doesn't like to feel revulsion and guilt? Unable to see clearly this moment what is taking place around and within us, we blame ourselves and others, and we think about more desirable ways of reacting. Compassion then remains an idea that induces emotions, including guilt, and the desire to do something good.

I may send compassionate thoughts toward others, or do charitable things for them and thereby feel more worthy, less guilty. Is that compassion? Is compassion an idea, an intention, a feeling, a training, a reaction? Does it want results? Does it have anything to do with the sense of "self" and "other?"

Maybe it is impossible to *know* what compassion is. Do you see what I mean? When I think I'm compassionate, I'm really not. Compassion is not self-reflecting, self-serving. It operates freely, unself-consciously only when this whole memory/thought circuit of self-centeredness is in abeyance. Then there is undivided energy to see nonjudgmentally what it is in human beings like you and me, rich or poor, that causes suffering, revulsion, and guilt and what is behind the yearning for compassionate action to end it all. Compassion needs no thinker, no doer, no knower, no giver or receiver, to function in its mysterious ways.

Your other question is, why is impermanence a source of liberation and joy at one time, and at other times it is distressing and depressing? Let's look. As in our examination of compassion, we ask, "Is impermanence an idea?" Ideas have effects on this organism. They create moods, and, depending on the way I feel when the idea arises, the effects on my mood may vary.

For instance, if I feel miserable, the idea "All is impermanent" may well trigger hopeful thoughts that my misery won't last forever. Hopeful thoughts arouse pleasant chemical reactions throughout the body that may be experienced and interpreted as joy and liberation from misery. If, however, while savoring feelings of joy, thoughts arise that joy too is impermanent, these may create a depressive mood. Can we examine all this quietly, spaciously?

I rarely talk about "impermanence" because one easily gets caught in concepts. If there is open awareness of *what is* from moment to moment, there is only that.

A tree with bare branches in winter, fragrant blossoms in spring, dark green leaves in summer, and colorful foliage in autumn is always just what it is. An oak crashing to the ground during an ice storm is only that. A decaying log is what it is. Thinking connects memories to create the idea of "impermanence."

Where is impermanence this very instant?

Helping Others

Can I be unconditionally with you in the presence of sorrow,
fear, or whatever? Can I be fully understanding of the deep
desire to get rid of it all, without knowing what to do about it,
without depending on a technique, just letting it all happen?

In the midst of a retreat, or during one's ordinary daily life, there may
be a sudden opening, an insight. One doesn't know the why or where-
fore, but such moments are not marked by conflict, pettiness, or fear.
Everything is just as it is. Nothing is missing. Nothing is special. There
is truly no one separate, no separate thing. There is the joy and
sparkling aliveness of everything. One would like to share this, but
what is there to share?

Now someone in the grip of fear, pain, or sorrow comes for help.
Can one be of help?

Being together, is one simply there with what is manifesting in both
of us this moment, letting it unfold as it will? Or does one bring up concepts like, "There is no self to be afraid" or "Fear and sorrow are essentially empty"? To suggest to someone caught up in fear or pain that he
or she relate to this from a space of "no-self" or "emptiness" would deny
what needs to be felt fully and listened to patiently, without judging.

Saying to someone, "Your fear and sorrow are empty illusions," is not
being completely with what we call fear and sorrow. Even labelling something "fear" is already a step away from the real thing. To be there completely with whatever is going on inwardly, and outwardly, do we need to
"know" it at all? What is there when naming and knowing are absent?

Do we need to use any special techniques when entering into sorrow
and fear? An appropriate response can come directly, unpremeditated-
ly, out of open, silent listening and looking together, without knowing.

This chapter stems in part from a Springwater Center Newsletter *article of*
October 1991 but has been rewritten for publication here.

What this response will be in any given situation we do not know and cannot plan. It is not an intellectual talking about the emptiness or illusion of self. Rather the response emerges from a quiet presence in the midst of everything that is unfolding this very instant, out of the stillness of not wanting or resisting anything.

Feelings and emotions do seem very solid when we're caught up in them, and we are all habituated to express or repress them, escape from them, or want to do something about the mental and physical distress they cause. Can I be unconditionally with you in the presence of sorrow, fear, or whatever? Can I be fully understanding of the deep desire to get rid of it all, without knowing what to do about it, without depending on a technique, just letting it all happen? Everything is right here to be discovered, seen, felt, and listened to openly, gently, as the splattering rain, the passing clouds, and the songs of birds.

The words that are spoken by one person may not be understood by the other this instant, but something much deeper than words is functioning when the mind is not caught up in fearing or wanting anything, or even the desire to help.

End of Retreat

A week of silent retreat has ended, come and gone in a flash, like the winds gusting wildly last evening, blowing through everything, blowing the trees, the hair, the clothes, bending the cattails along the edge of the pond, whipping the water into ripples, streaks, and waves in patterns dark and light with furious joy.

Awakening this morning to utter brilliance and calm. Golden sun rising over the autumn hills close and clear, each blade of grass, each window pane shimmering brightly with pearls of water and light. Clouds of ever changing color and form floating across a vast open sky that does not move at all—that does not mind, or know, recall, or want anything.

These were Toni's closing words at the end of a retreat in Springwater, autumn 1992.